LIFE IS NOT A
SPECTATOR SPORT

LIFE IS NOT A SPECTATOR SPORT

How to get it on with life, rather than just getting by

By
Art McNeil

Syndicated columnist, keynote speaker, humorist, best selling author, entrepreneur and executive advisor, Art McNeil has established an international reputation for helping people move beyond inspiration and knowing-to doing.

Art is a North American success story, founding The Achieve Group whose namesake, Achieve Global, has become the largest training company in the world.

His syndicated column uses insight, humor and family values to get people off the couch and onto life's playing field-building stronger relationships, caring families, supportive communities and successful careers.

Art's writings and speaking engagements consistently receive excellent reviews from a broad range of audiences.

Canadian Catalogue in Publication Data

McNeil, Art

Life is not a Spectator Sport: how to get it on with life rather than just getting by

Includes index.
ISBN 0-9681590-1-X

1. Success. 2. Interpersonal relations. I. Title.

BJ1581.2.M254 1999   158   C99-900885-4

Cover design by graphic-zone.com
Photography by Art McNeil

This book is dedicated to Fuzz and Lucy

"Thanks for your gift of love, values and room to grow."

Dear Reader,

Success is in the eye of the beholder. Therefore, one's quality of life should be judged only by the person who is being assessed. Who is happy, who is better off, who is winning and who cares about being in the race? Where there is life there can be no absolutes.

My experience suggests that position, wealth and talent; have little to do with personal satisfaction. How you go about living, day in and day out, is every bit as important as achievement-perhaps more so.

I've been blessed with opportunities to study both winners and losers. Working several continents and meeting people from many walks of life has taught me that a life well lived, is humanity's crowning glory.

This book offers a distillation of my discoveries through the eyes of a child; son, husband, father, grandfather, friend, brother, student, executive, consultant and late-age behavioral science enthusiast.

Trying to positively influence the human condition is my passion. This book is an expression of my unswerving love of life-yours, theirs and mine.

During the writing process I received more than a little help from editor Jim Merriam, wife Judy, readers of my weekly column, family members and friends.

Thanks everybody,

Art McNeil

Index by Category

"Stories may appear under more than one heading"

Introduction:
(Part A) Personal development
Taking the lead:

Learning from the experience:

Laughing at yourself ; a growth strategy:

(Part B) Making the people side of life work:

Developing sound relationships:

Communicating for clearer understanding:

Community building:

Making the Connection

If you have an insight or a personal experience that you would like to share, I'd love to hear from you. I learn and grow from your feedback. Email to art@artmcneil.com

If you enjoy these stories, drop a line to your local, daily or weekly newspaper editor. That way we could connect each week through my syndicated column "Life is not a spectator sport".

Add a motivational series of 'Life is not a Spectator Sport' to your company newsletter.

If your organization has a newsletter, inform the editor that I offer a special 'motivational' series of my syndicated column. The columns, distributed by email, are ready to print. Save time and provide your readers with cost effective access to performance enhancing insights and information that is world-class. For more information or to order, visit
http://www.achieverscatalyst.com/life.htm on the internet.

Table of Contents

I went for a walk in the rain last night. That doesn't sound like a significant event, but it was. I had just completed a 2-year writing project; E mailing the manuscript into production 20 minutes before deadline.

WALKING IN THE RAIN

My old english teacher Miss Brown would have scored this close call a major accomplishment as my essays and book reports were notoriously late. The task ended well after midnight. During the home stretch my dog started nosing into my business. She has a habit of slipping her snout under my forearm to get attention. That night her intrusions were particularly annoying because they were screwing up my typing. The last line of the last page of my new book contains her contribution. #nl;ku means, "my bladder is about to explode and I need a walk-right now!"

Once the E mail was complete, I turned off the computer and started down the stairs. Kayla bolted past me doing a 5 point, turning-skid (her bum was dragging) on the hardwood floor before crashing into the door. "She must really have to go," I thought guiltily. It was raining so I took an umbrella from my golf bag, naively assuming it would cover the both of us.

As soon as the dog hit fresh air she broke heel and headed for the long grass. I trained her not to fancy short grass squatting, hoping to keep our lawn free of those unsightly yellow bulls-eyes that differentiates the owners of female K9s. Our lawn is usually open season for Kayla because I am such a procrastinator when it comes to doing yard work.

After her business was complete, she went crashing through low hanging vegetation like a mad-dog and had a ball mucking about in puddles on the road. She was oblivious to the rain, sniffing anything that moved and some disgusting stuff that hadn't moved in a long time. By contrast, I was huddled under what amounted to a portable tent emblazoned with a Coors beer logo. For some reason I was afraid I'd melt if I got wet.

I don't know what set me off, but I suddenly felt incredibly free and alive. I discarded the umbrella and went face up into the falling rain. I was peppered with thousands of little slaps. It felt so good I shouted "thanks, I needed that," to no one in particular. It was wringing wet out there, but the evening was warm and the air was full of fresh smells and sounds I'd long forgotten. To Kayla's delight, we even splashed around in a huge puddle together. I dry off much easier than my dog, yet getting wet doesn't phase her in the least.

How many delightful walks have I missed? How could I forget the sight, sound, feel and smell of a warm summer rain? More importantly, how many other opportunities (to experience life's intimacy and passion) am I missing?

I don't know about cats but when it starts raining dogs, I'm joining in the fun from here on in.

"TIME'S FUN WHEN YOU'RE HAVING FLIES"

-an old frog

I take in the odd ballgame these days. I don't expect to catch flies anymore but I am having fun reliving flights of past fancy when I too, engaged the delightful game of baseball. I've relaxed my participation only rule and become a spectator because my grandsons are playing on the same team. Their pairing is peculiar because of the age spread-Dylan is 4 and Jacob 8. There weren't enough little people to form a complete team, so Jake was asked to join his younger brother. Mother makes him attend every game anyway so it wasn't much of a sacrifice.

The "T" ball league has no pitcher. Rather, the ball is struck as it sits on a stationary Tee at home base. The kids wear oversized T-shirts that often resemble ankle length dresses. All of the players are cute as buttons as they struggle valiantly to master the game's complex rules and challenging skills. Everything is pretty much laid-back at this level and everybody has a good time.

Rather than assume the traditional defensive positions of baseball, tot players socialize when they play the field. Our team congregates around second base. It's like a hot stove league until a ball rolls by. Then they all charge after it. Most plays conclude in a massive tumble scrum as teammates fight for possession. Nobody (except for a few frustrated parents) pays much attention to base runners who oft-times miss their signals. One little charmer having made it to third base, responded to her coach's enthusiastic directive, "run home!" by doing exactly that. She was out of the park and two blocks down the road before her father caught up.

I recently acquired an unorthodox assignment as the team water-boy. It started when Dylan, after drinking 5 glasses of liquid, was caught short in center field. Unceremoniously holding his privates (tough to do when wearing a baseball mitt), he started jumping up and down. His inactive leg was curled like climbing ivy around the busy one. "Pappa!" he wailed, "I've got to pee-right now!" The compassionate umpire called a time-out and hand in hand, my grandson and I headed for the heads. The play drew a standing ova-tion, the first I've ever received in baseball. Our fluid problem must have been contagious because the whole team went down-one at a time. I received a week's worth of exercise that night, running ball players with big thirsts and pint sized bladders to the loo.

Tots "T" ball activity is worth its weight in gold because behind the spontaneous frivolity, many of life's most important lessons are being learned. I picked up on the following:

- Pay attention to what you are doing.
- There are consequences to inaction as well as action.
- Never give up (even if you've been heading in the wrong direc-tion).
- Don't be afraid to try; mistakes are the foundation of success.
- Trust the counsel of respected others when the rules aren't mak-ing sense.
- When games are run well, everybody can win.
- Never assume that people will interpret an instruction the same way.
- What you take in, comes out and you can't always control the timing.
- In a tight squeeze, don't be afraid to ask for help.

"Batman has become a powerful icon representing the dominance of good over evil. My association with bats has failed to foster anything close to the behavior of a superhero." Art

Real life periodically produces hilarious scenarios that no TV sitcom could ever hope to capture. This attempt at documenting one such episode does not do it justice. I wish you could have been there.

A BAT OUT OF HELL

Act #1 The first time it happened was on a comfortable old couch at the family cottage. A young lady, who would eventually become my wife, stretched her lithe body and contentedly flipped the pages of a romance novel. Across the room, on a second sofa, I slipped in and out of consciousness.

Sporadic waking moments were split between watching a baseball game and wistfully observing the light of my life. Together, we basked in the tranquillity of a warm summer evening. Suddenly, a piercing scream jolted me to full alert. Across the room, shapely legs were frantically pumping the air and my fiancée's face was smothered in a pillow. I was mentally racing through first aid options when the victim finally ran out of oxygen. Burning lungs were filled by one gigantic gulp followed by, "There's a bat in here!" I rushed to her defense as a terrifying shadow missed my head by inches. "An erratic bat is on the loose and you are so very close to an exit", my churning mind repeated. Instinct took over as I unceremoniously bolted from the cottage. "Get outta there," I shouted over my shoulder as the screen door slammed shut.

It took a great deal of time and effort to recover from what was a most cowardly display. But amends were made and I was forgiven. In spite my shortcomings in the gallantry department, we eventually married.

Act #2 The scene is 30 years later. My sister and her children are visiting. Kayla, our golden retriever is sleeping contentedly at the hearth. The time is 10 p.m. and our guests are in bed. The Mrs. Herself is busy securing doors downstairs as your humble servant wraps-up another evening shift at the computer. Suddenly, I am shaken by an ear splitting scream, "there's a bat in here!" It was de ja vu all over again. I executed a knee jerk retreat to the safety of a locked bathroom.

This time my conscience was operating with Jesuit authority. The thought of failing at bat a second time was more than I could bear so something had to be done. I mustered every remaining ounce of courage and slinked my way to a storage closet down the hall. Girding my loins with whatever I could find, I cautiously descended to the main floor battlefield-armed with a tennis racket, window screen and the protective covering of a bed sheet.

The Mrs. Herself was shouting encouragement from under the kitchen table. Sister ingeniously used our two line telephone system and phoned in support from an upstairs bedroom. Her kids took up a forward observation post in the hall closet. It was a Battle of Britain style dog fight as the bat skillfully dodged my best backhands and numerous forehand strokes. Clearly, my offensive strategy was not working and I was running out of adrenaline. I opened all the doors and windows and took up a defensive position under the table beside my unimpressed spouse.

After what seemed an eternity, the bat landed within inches of an open dining room door. "We have him," I gloated. Anticipating victory, the kids cheered from behind closed closet doors and the second phone line started ringing. I charged from under the table bellowing at the top of my lungs. The plan was to drive out the bat but unfortunately my scream terrified Kayla who, abandoning six months of obedience training, peed on the hardwood floor while running on the spot. The bat eventually made it to safety, our family inherited an indelible memory and my honor was restored. Well, almost.

"People enjoy reflecting on pleasant or humorous experiences. Let's leave the past and have a look at how humans perceive the future." Art

You've heard that voice before. The boo bird on your shoulder that always thinks the worst. How many times have you hesitated when you should have gone for it? Why is the knee jerk response of most people, to initially view opportunity as a negative?

THE SPACE I HAVE BETWEEN MY EARS

Humans are born with an awesome space between their ears. Teachers unkindly referred to mine with great regularity. They meant to demean but were actually paying me a great compliment. Nature hates empty spaces and works hard to keep them filled. It is the phenomenal capacity of the human brain to fill empty space with imagined possibilities that differentiates us from the rest of earth's creatures. Whether we like it or not, our minds are obsessively painting pictures of possible futures 24 hours a day. Mental pictures are important because a large determinant of how you choose to behave, is your conscious or below conscious expectation of what the future holds in store. We are predisposed to move towards whatever our minds dwell on. Think the worst or the best, and it will probably happen.

According to the late Dr. Ron Lippitt, people are programmed negatively before the age of five. Your well intentioned parents, older siblings, friends and other family members, left you with an outlook on life conditioned to a ratio of 12:1 negative and that's if you are average.

An example of unintentional negative programming took place each Sunday in my childhood home. Mornings were always hectic. I would race down the stairs and bolt for the door. Typically, I'd get the hook seconds before freedom. Mother would unceremoniously pin me down with one knee and use both hands to comb my unruly hair. I could never get it right. She unintentionally conditioned me to believe that the family's reputation was resting squarely on my head.

To this day, prior to taking the stage during speaking engagements, I often experience a nagging feeling that something isn't right. First I do a very discreet fly check. Once that primary concern has been eliminated, I start worrying about my hair. A mature adult in my mid 50's and I'm still at the mercy of an inner voice saying, "go out looking like that and you'll scare the neighbors."

Lippit's negative ratio means that left to our own devices we can expect as many as 12 negative images before we'll see a single positive. And not all mental pictures are experienced consciously. Subconscious negatives are troublesome because they leave us feeling uncomfortable without knowing why. One evening my daughter returned home with a young man who had an eight-pound bowling ball dangling from his left ear. I don't remember seeing a mental picture, but my stomach did. It started squirting battery acid the second I laid eyes on him. Perhaps the space between my ears imagined me walking my daughter down the aisle- towards this interesting person.

You can avoid the undisciplined chatter of a negatively programmed mind. Just keep head spaces filled with positive pictures. A productive mindset is accomplished by imagining a preferred future. The alternative is to accept negativity because head space will fill based on prior conditioning. Paint yourself a picture of what it would be like if things worked out perfectly. Don't worry about being considered naïve or overly optimistic because at 12:1, a few positive thoughts will only level the playing field. One final word on the topic-"where there is no vision, the people perish."- Proverbs 29:18

"Imagine acquiring a mindset that makes you a winner every time. Football great, Coach Vince Lombardi was quoted as saying he never accepted the loss of a game. Rather, he advised teams that their mistake was running out of time. The bottom line to his message is that success is inevitable when you have the right attitude. After experiencing failure, it is tempting to admit defeat and give up on any thought of improvement." Art

MY DIDGERIDOO DON'T

One of the few benefits of working internationally is the opportunity to connect with informed locals who delight in exposing backyard secrets to the uninformed. It is quite different from being at the mercy of an overstated brochure created in the bowels of Holiday Inn's home office.

During one such business trip, friends introduced me to many of Australia's endearing places, inhabitants and customs. Peculiarity is the order of the day down under. There are trees that retain leaves and shed bark and Kualas are not bears at all, but dim witted, leaf eaters that move with the speed of a disgruntled postal worker. Australia is also the last bastion of male chauvinism, perhaps because their gene pool is primarily British and criminal.

It was the music of indigenous people that defined this enchanting continent for me. The didgeridoo is to Australia, what the banjo is to North America. This revered folk instrument is made from a hollowed out tree root. The sound is primal and captivating. In impact it compares to North America's wilderness icon, the plaintive wail of a loon.

I pride myself on being a jack of all musical instruments, yet master of none. I'd never met a noise-maker I couldn't blow, pick, pound or strum - until I was introduced to the didgeridoo. Try as I might, my didjeridoo don't.

Unlike traditional wind instruments, a didjeridoo player uses not only lips but most of the face. The instrument resonates with a distinctive droning sound; who-ong, who-ong (I hope you heard that) and the player's cheeks flap like dog lips hanging out of a car window at 90 miles an hour. I tried to play this Australian classic but after hundreds of attempts, the best I could do was to silently pass wind. On my way home I crossed the international dateline a beaten man.

The following year my friend attended a conference at my Canadian retreat center. The price I set for his admission was to import one of those troublesome instruments. I had secretly vowed to sound the didgeridoo or blow myself away trying. My friend, always thoughtful and courteous, included an instructional tape. Typically Australian, the first lesson was to blow a continuous stream of bubbles through a straw into a mug of beer; while at the same time breathing in through your nose. Few master the art of continuous blowing but the natural human propensity to suck, renders many a student inebriated after long hours of arduous practice. Needless to say, I have not progressed beyond the first lesson.

"I showed my wife a rational article as to why males can't help being poor listeners. She read thoughtfully and started talking about how the concept made her feel. Similar to my inability to blow the didgeridoo, it would appear I am genetically predisposed to blow my conversations with women." Art

YES DEAR, I'M LISTENING

I have a long history of failure when it comes to communicating with women. Two sisters, a couple of grown daughters, my wife and the family dog speak in a secret estrogen based code. It's a language I pretend to understand but seldom do.

I am accused regularly of not listening by the women in my life so by popular request, I had my hearing checked. The audiologist said I could experience some difficulty hearing feminine voices at the high end of the human speaking range. When I asked for a letter to confirm these findings, she closed gender ranks and refused to give me what could have been a valuable "get out of jail free" pass.

There may be a valid reason other than a hearing defect, as to why men seldom live up to the communication expectations of the fairer sex.

According to pop psychologists, women are natural communicators. They have the uncanny ability of understanding through intuition, what others are trying to say. For example, my wife completes sentences for me. What's really scary is that she is usually accurate about what is going on in my head.

In ancient times, women were assigned the clan's critical gathering role. They collected berries, nuts, grains and other commodities from Nature's extensive garden. Female finders developed the skill of scanning entire landscapes. They were trained to look behind, in front and from side to side in order to locate food. The most successful gatherers were those with the broadest scope. Women still use the "entire landscape" perspective when communicating. They need to discuss feelings and want to investigate the margins of every issue. Before enlightenment, I unwisely called this process "beating around the bush".

Ancestral males by contrast, focused on bringing home the bacon. They were red meat hunters and evolved quite differently. Over many centuries, men developed the skill of zeroing in on a specific target. Success demanded the segregation of one beast from other possibilities. Then the hunters were conditioned to act quickly without a second thought. Successful hunters made life and death decisions impassionately. Modern man is no different. During the process of listening, he will latch on to whatever he initially perceives as "the problem." An annoying side effect of this genetic trait is that once locked on, he becomes oblivious to everything else.

Men instinctively view their job as solving specific problems. Marginal dialogue (feelings et al) conflict with his goal. It will be difficult for uninformed male readers to comprehend but women actually prefer the "feeling" of being heard, over being offered a viable solution.

Ladies, if you want to improve communications with the men in your life; get their attention by letting them know specifically what you want at the beginning of the conversation. Get rid of unproductive salutations such as "honey." Start with a red meat attention getter. "Hunter, I don't want a solution here. What I need is for you to really listen." Once you've got his attention, hold it with more clarity i.e. "You will be successful if at the end of this conversation I feel heard. Until I give the word, your ideas and opinions are out of bounds"

Good hunting ladies.

"Communication is an essential life skill. Rediscovering how to play is equally powerful when it comes to building and maintaining solid relationships. If the dialogue at home or at work skews toward the serious, nobody will be learning or having fun." Art

TRANSFORMING THE HOUSE THAT PAPA BUILT

Our large home on the shores of beautiful Georgian Bay doubles as an executive learning center. But of late, protocol, management reserve and strategic thinking have given way to raucous behaviour and spontaneous merriment that can shift to troubled anxiety and back in the blink of an eye.

This transformation is happening because (under the direction of 4 grandchildren, 2 daughters, their husbands, my sisters and brothers in law, Grandma Lucy, a few good friends and last but not least our mildew scented dog who won't stay out of the lake) a new dimension has been added to this once tranquil establishment.

At this writing I am in recovery from yet another long weekend at Futures on Georgian, known affectionately in our family circle as Nanny and Papa's house. Once an exclusive center for executive retreats, it has been transformed to accommodate the family attack. And to this road weary consultant, the transition feels great. Here's what I've learned since my gang started remodeling:

- Children are not as inhibited as executives. They are willing to let go and are not afraid to fill their diapers with unwanted stuff. Once enlightened, children move on quickly without guilt or shame, ready to consume again. Management meetings often produce a similar output. Mature conferees are less willing however, to part with heavy loads. Many pretend they have not digested anything and that movement is neither desirable nor necessary. They get all bunged up trying to maintain the status quo and often take unwanted stuff home. Adults, like children when the output process is restricted, whine a lot and take in less. Anal retentives (sometimes called hangers on) are often slow learners. Children know you won't grow until you throw.

- A recurring issue at our house is who will sleep with whom. Our grandkids have established the disruptive convention of bedding down with Nanny. This ritual leaves Papa somewhat grumpy. More serious problems arise however, when a gaggle of grand kids visit at the same time. With the discipline of a well prepared class action suit, they all lay claim to the master's bedroom. On these occasions, Papa makes his own retreat and moves to an isolated mother in law suite designed originally for the use of visiting instructors.

- Children, experimenting around our kitchen table with self glorification, power plays and manipulations, eerily resemble executive conferees who engage in more subtle forms of intimidation. The only difference between the conferees and our grandkids, is genuineness and the size of their words.

Interesting people from all over the world visit our home and participate in a plethora of learning experiences. I have gained much from each and every one of them. But it's the grandchildren who have helped the Mrs. Herself and me rediscover that uninhibited play is not only enjoyable, it is nature's most powerful teaching aid. My grandkids also give better hugs than uptight management conferees and never tire of listening to my silly stories.

"When I suffer writer's block I visit a local library or bookstore. Surrounded by thousand of books, I feel supported and encouraged by the authors who obviously stuck to their knitting and made things happen." Art

FOR THE LOVE OF READING

A good book can return me to the security of mother's knee; recreate historic battles, expose me to intimate moments between lovers, propel me to far off galaxies and at a more practical level, keep me out of harms way. In my world, reading is not a pastime nor is it passive. I participate by imagining faces, colors, shapes, sounds, places and smells. Characters created by the author are recreated in my mind's eye and often earn my genuine affection, anger or loathing. Ending an engaging novel can leave me feeling like I'm bidding farewell to an old friend for the last time.

Watching TV or a movie is different than the experience of reading a book. In the old days the variance was less because directors knew how to titillate the imagination of their audience, using emotion and innuendo. TV and movie viewing has become more consumptive and less creative. The adrenaline rush caused by action sequences has replaced imagination and relegated movie going to a second rate spectator sport. This shift is transforming, values driven human beings into lower order reactives, who respond mindlessly and predictably like sharks to external stimuli. Our out of control entertainment industry is encouraging violence by desensitizing people and catering to our primal instincts rather than promoting civilized thought.

Using TV as a baby sitter may help kids and parents pass the time, but sitting in front of a tube anesthetizes small minds that should be exploring and learning from the experience. Children living in environments that repress creativity with too much TV viewing are often depressed. In extreme cases they will be scarred for life. Reading by contrast, engages and challenges the mind. It is an extremely creative activity.

Taking the time to read stories to a child is a gift second only to the essentials such as love, shelter, food and security. Sitting on the knee of a caring adult, the child makes physical, emotional and spiritual contact. They have an uncanny ability to pick up on expressed emotion so it is important to really get into what is being read. Children taught to love books are also learning to love themselves, others and life in general.

Many adults slipped through the cracks of our educational system and never learned to read. The majority of illiterate adults were never read to as children. By the time they reached school age they were far behind. Reading is a cornerstone of learning. Early exposure to books makes this essential skill enjoyable and as natural as breathing. A child denied the shared reading experience is in reality an abused child, saddled forever with a crippling and unnecessary handicap. If you love books, volunteer as a reading coach and help stamp out illiteracy in your community. There are adults wanting to reclaim their right to literacy. Neglected preschoolers could use your support as well.

"I was shattered when confronted with the reality that my family would never get it together like the Waltons. Who would have thought a black bear would pull the trigger on my naïve fantasy. So long John boy." Art

For some reason, my destiny seems to include black bears. I am not a wilderness person. Seldom traveling off the beaten track, I prefer the company of human beings to wild hairy things. So it's not natural that Euarctos Americanus and I should meet with such regularity. Something more than mere coincidence must be at work because each encounter has produced a valuable insight.

BEARLY SURVIVING

On the first occasion I was traveling through the Rocky Mountains with my wife, our two girls and an Irish setter named Megan. We were hauling a small tent camper, with a wind up roof. My gang had just hit the road after grudgingly vacating a comfortable motel room. I am not a natural naturalist and was pulling the trailer for emergency use only. A few miles down the road, a heavy fog set in. I evoked wagon master privileges and pulled into a scenic outlook station at the side of the road rather than accept my family's suggestion that we return to the motel. I cranked up the camper top, ignited a propane stove and sat back contentedly as The Mrs. Herself cranked out a mess of bacon and eggs. Fresh, mountain air made the food smell and taste wonderful. It was raining outside but we were together, snug and dry. Crammed around the camper table, I fantasized that we were just like the Walton's.

Our Rocky Mountain high didn't last for several reasons. First, sharing space with preteen sisters who had been confined together for two weeks, and were ready to kill each other. Second, having a wet dog underfoot that wanted out every ten seconds. (Megan's bladder was the size of a pea.) And finally, a seething wife who was showing no signs of forgiving me for vacating our comfortable motel room. After breakfast, an angry din replaced the stony silence. It was obviously time to move on so I gallantly dispatched everybody to the car and in the pouring rain, started closing up the camper. I erroneously assumed that sympathy would provide a foundation for making amends.

I was wet, ornery and having a tough time folding canvas while at the same time, trying to lower the camper roof. I felt hot breath on my neck and shouted (in hindsight, most unpleasantly), "don't just stand there, give me a hand!" It became obvious that no help would be forthcoming so I turned to express my disappointment. Staring me right in the eye was not the love of my life but a huge black bear. The beast actually grinned at me.

I was in the final stages of preparing to meet my maker when Megan the wonder dog appeared out of nowhere. Her courageous charge was most peculiar because she was running in mid-piddle, probably from fright. Her ploy worked and the disgruntled bear was driven into the woods. I looked towards heaven and the family car, seeking whatever support I could find. In unison four door locks clicked shut. "This would never happen to the Walton's, I mused."

Bear episode #2

My family wanted to share our newfound affection for the Rocky Mountains with my visiting parents from the east. Exposure to a full cycle (from sunrise to sunset, through dark of night and on to a second sunrise) is required before you can really appreciate the full majesty of a mountain range. So we took off towing a tent trailer that could almost accommodate the Mrs. Herself, our two daughters, my parents, an Irish setter and me (provided the girls were getting along and it didn't rain). With six people, food, camping equipment and a neurotic dog barking at passing vehicles, our trip was intimate from the onset.

We arrived at a campsite that offered giant pine trees, a cascading river and a plethora of spring flowers. Wrangled nerve ends were quickly soothed by the sight, sound and smells of Mother Nature in full bloom. A wilderness dinner, consisting of hot dogs, pork and beans and freshly caught trout was soon laid before us. The meal's only detraction was a 5 year-old who wouldn't speak to us because we were eating a potential addition to her aquarium. After watching a magnificent sunset and singing a few campfire tunes, 7 contented souls retired for the night.

The evening's tranquility was shattered by a volley of violent bangs under our camper. The kids flew from their upper bunk, executing perfect paratrooper rolls as they landed on my back. Megan went into a full point with her front paw planted firmly in my ear. My parents were sack racing across the floor in sleeping bags. With weight shifting to one side, our camper starting to tip. I quickly vaulted my 200 pounds plus into the vacated space to stabilize the situation inside. But outside, events were very much out of control. Mother was screaming, father stood beside the door brandishing a broom, man's best friend was howling like a coon hound and my wife was consoling the girls from the bottom of a communal sleeping bag. "Shut up!" I finally shouted in frustration. "Don't talk to your mother like that!" our 5 year old retorted, glaring at me with tiny hands turned outwards on her hips. To break the silence I mumbled, "she's a clone of her mother." I cautiously peeked out the window and discovered the source of our chagrin. A huge black bear was slapping a metal cooler around like a basketball. I shouted unceremoniously to adjoining campsites, "does anybody know how to get rid of a bear?"

A bearded good Samaritan appeared out of nowhere. He was dressed in the traditional garb of mountain men, a classical pair of red long underwear accentuated by hiking boots and a baseball cap worn backwards. In spite of the chaos, Mother vividly recalls, "his back flap was definitely open." Our savior swung an axe and screamed at the top of his lungs, "get out of here you (expletives deleted)." The bear obligingly turned in his tracks and made for the hills. Our courageous neighbor disappeared without a word and once again the night was silent, except for my daughter lecturing me about the necessity of people, "even at your age Dad, " respecting their elders. Mother agreed.

"Myths like the Walton family are seldom reality based. Nor is a common erroneous assumption about the value of equal treatment." Art

Every human being develops a pattern of behavior, a preferred method of going about getting things done. When you are doing things your own way, relationship tension for you will be low. But if the people you are interacting with have a different behavioral style, their tension will be higher.

TO ASK OR TO TELL

-communicating
with extroverts
and introverts

Relationship tension typically has a negative impact on results and can create conflict. Recognizing the behavioral pattern of yourself and others allows you to manage relationship tension by modifying your contribution. The golden rule, "do unto others as you would have them do unto you," is helpful in terms of selecting a desired outcome. But when it comes to interacting with others a more productive rule might be, "do unto others as they would prefer to be done unto."

In the grand scheme of things there seems to be an even split along the lines of behavioral style. Behavioral style is each person's unique way of going about getting things done. For example, my wife gets things done by asking questions. I navigate life primarily in the telling mode. Convention has it that telling puts me in a more powerful position. Not so! The Mrs. Herself can ask a simple questions such as, "Art, do you enjoy living here?" and etch in my mind, pictures worth a least a thousand words.

Askers are introverts who process things internally. They prefer the tranquillity and precision of their own mind over the undisciplined chatter of a noisy group. When askers finally do speak, their thoughts are usually well constructed and complete. Introverts typically resent anybody messing with their output because it is offered as a finished product. Introverts go inside to process data.

Telling extroverts are groupies by nature. They do their best thinking out loud and in a crowd. Success means getting everybody's stuff out on the table. The personal thoughts of self and others are never considered complete or sacred, just more grist for the mill. Extroverts expect others to roll up their sleeves and massage ideas until the finished product emerges. Extroverts go outside to process data.

Extroverts frequently write off introverts because so little information is offered during the idea generation stage of a meeting. Conflict may also appear later in the process if the introvert's completed thought is not taken seriously or considered communal property by the group.

Styles are calibrated differently in terms of emotional display. Because introverts process internally, they often appear slow, less volatile and more in control of their feelings. There is seldom any external warning that introverts are upset. They almost never get mad but will often get even.

Extroverts by contrast, are the squeaky wheels of society. In group settings they demand and usually get more than their fair share of air time. They consider emotional outbursts normal and soon forget disruptions, unlike introverts who, because they keep things bottled up inside, are more apt to harbor a lingering resentment.

The next time you are working in a group, remember that emotion (mad; sad glad etc.) has many faces. Don't make the mistake of assuming that external displays are an accurate indicator of the intensity of a person's feelings. Consider behavioral style and use the natural strength of each group member appropriately.

Tension during family interaction can also be reduced once members understand that behavioral differences are not necessarily a variance of opinion or attitude. For example, my Aunt Ruby always hugged and kissed my sisters and me. Greetings were usually a wild display of emotion that left smeared lipstick on blushing cheeks. The greetings of my Aunt Ruth were quite different. She asked grown up questions and displayed her emotion with a gentle pat to the head. I felt cared for by both.

"Feeling valued is a basic human need. Before the written word our primitive ancestors embraced a survival process that modern society has forgotten. Elders and children may hold the key to our achieving a moral and ethical renaissance."
Art

ELDERS AND THE CHILDREN

Do you have fond memories of your grandparents or other older people? I remember receiving special treatment from the elders in my life. Unlike parents who must discipline and provide the essentials of life, elders are free to offer children unconditional affection and support. Today's highly mobile nuclear family may be creating problems by limiting exposure to older adults.

Studies of the human brain identified that seniors and children have a chemical makeup not shared by the middle generation, the segment of society capable of reproduction. Looking at my behavior as a teenager, the difference makes sense. Puberty was the start of turbulence in my life as it is for most people. Perhaps it was a chemical reaction that took one last run at me during mid life. Unlike my first crisis, the latter was fortunately mundane and uneventful.

The fact that adult brains are chemically different from children and seniors, makes for some interesting speculation. Consider that before the written word, elders held the crucial responsibility of passing spiritual beliefs, history and tribal customs on to the third generation. They worked with children every day, telling stories and playing games designed to build a sense of shared values and strong visions of a positive future.

While adults were coping with here-and-now essentials such as food, shelter, safety and procreation; lessons from the past were used by elders to shape young imaginations and develop positive expectations. Could chemical similarity and a generation skip in child rearing responsibility be a forgotten but essential component of human survival?

Today, parents do the child rearing themselves or they assign the job to daycare workers and teachers. Unfortunately, these people are usually members of a chemically altered middle generation. Here-and-now oriented adults may be less capable when it comes to teaching values and developing spirituality. The rampant materialism of this century started when the industrial revolution broke up the multi-generation family unit. Our increasingly decadent society may be suffering because elders are no longer charged with passing on non-material human essentials.

The presence of children has been shown to slow down and even reverse senility. Could this be another variation of the adage "use it or lose it?" We may unwittingly, be relegating an essential development resource to childless retirement communities and nursing homes. Rather than the perennial problem we assume it to be, the generation gap may be an underutilized societal asset.

"The world needs leaders from every age group. But what is leadership exactly? It has always been a wooly subject that lacks the discipline of management. I have spent a large part of my professional life trying to clarify our understanding of leadership." Art

LEADERSHIP IS EVERY-BODY'S BUSINESS

In an attempt to understand the relationship between leaders and followers I found it helpful to differentiate the activity of leading from the position of managing. Management is about planning, staffing and control. It is a formal position. Leadership concerns itself with will to win and the desire to belong. The very term "to lead" implies having a place to go or a way of being that does not currently exist.

Society has been institutionalized to the extent that many of us are just managing to get by rather than exercising leadership over our own affairs. An example of being over managed is the complexity of minor sports such as Little league baseball. For the children who participate, there is no spontaneity, choosing of teams or having to sort out their own problems. Everything is done for them in typically adult fashion. Subsequently, much of the fun is gone from the game.

Managing means accepting the status quo and living by the rules within existing boundaries and constraints. Leadership not only focuses on getting the job done, it takes the initiative around the margins of an assignment to make things better. In a family or any other organization, management is about roles such as being a manager, secretary, father or sister. Leadership, by contrast, is about the people behind their positions.

Effective people are leaders as well as managers. They deal in hope, striving not only to produce and survive but to imagine and continuously improve. As you manage this week's routine, take the initiative to make things better, create a mental image of a preferred future and help others paint themselves into your picture. You will be leading; even though your steps may be small.

The following leadership model is from my book, Leadership: The "I" of the Hurricane:

Vision and Values: (Where are we going and what do we believe in?) Great leaders talk about and live by core values that are in line with the beliefs of potential followers. As well, they offer others access to vision which provides an inspiring reason for being. The combination of shared values and vision binds people to a leader.

Signaling Skills: Ineffective leaders often fail because they say one thing while signaling contradictory messages through their actions. Actions really do speak louder than words.

Signals transmitted through a leader's action, provides evidence that the organization's vision and values are genuine. Leaders who lead by example command respect. When there is consistency between the demands and actions of a leader, followers are motivated to participate and do whatever it takes to transform vision into reality.

Before the age of five we learned most of what we need to know in order to survive. We discerned what is really important by observing people in power. Before our verbal skills were developed we watched big people do things-ignoring what Mom and Dad said and paying attention to what they did.

As organization members, adults are child-like at heart. They watch what leaders do and react to the behavior. When executives worry about numbers, the odds are that's what middle managers will be doing as well.

Challenge and Appropriate Leader Response: If you stay visible, painting clear mental pictures of a winning future, if you give clear, uncomplicated signals, people will catch your drift and help you make the improbable happen. Like signaling skills, a leader's readiness to encourage challenge and to respond appropriately has a multiplier effect. Each appropriate leader response (in line with vision and values) made under fire, heightens credibility. Soldiers respond to leaders who have been tested under battle conditions.

A Strategic Map for Leadership:

$$L = f\,(V1+V2)\frac{SS \text{ X ALR}}{C}$$

(L) Leadership is equal to the function of (V1), having a mental picture or vision of a place to go or way of being plus (V2) an awareness of underlying core values that you and a critical mass of potential followers within a system believe in, times (SS) the use of skills to send consistent signals through day-to-day behavior in a manner that models personal commitment to the vision and core values.

Effective leaders accept as a given that (C) challenge is a legitimate responsibility of all organization members. When challenges are met with (ALR) appropriate leader responses ("appropriate" meaning consistent with the vision and core values), energy is available for transfer to task. The process of altering balance between (C) and (ALR) as a means of reinforcing (V1) and (V2), therefore, is the essence of leadership.

"A healthy primary relationship stimulates learning but after a few years, complexities can set in and complicate growth. The following puts a new spin on the old saying, being hung out to dry." Art

THE UMEWE FACTOR

Healthy people continue growing until the day they die. That goes for relationships as well. Compare marriage to a clothesline. Each partner is the equivalent of a separate pole and their relationship resembles the line strung between two independent support structures. Like clotheslines, a marriage can only be as strong as the weakest of its three components.

Nothing contributes to happiness like a committed marriage that is working. It produces an excellent climate for the development of health and wellness. Instead of building a nourishing relationship, many couples slip into mind numbing routines that support little more than a basic existence. Remember the first time you fell in love? Hormones were dancing and there were no boundaries between you and your partner. You lived for each other. It was a fun time and you strutted around like peacocks with only your best feathers showing. A blissful hormonally induced trance kept the warts well hidden.

Inevitably, the initial glow of infatuation wears off even the most intimate relationship. Partners suddenly find themselves confronted with the trials and tribulations of daily living. Most people go into a painful withdrawal when they first confront their partner without the support of romantic love's endorphins. The termination of nature's barbiturate spawned the classic line, "the honeymoon must be over." The mellowing of passion goes hand in hand with increased responsibility and extended history. Unfortunately, this reality marks the beginning of the end for many couples. Rather than accept a normal maturation process, one or both partners starts drifting, in search of another hormone rush. Nothing looks as pathetic as a dysfunctional adult who abandons responsibility, giving up what he or she already has in the hopeless pursuit of a reclaimed youth. Relationships like people, must grow to survive. Advancement towards maturity begins when youthful passion and spontaneity melds with the power of disciplined thinking. When healthy balance is achieved a good relationship fosters personal development.

Relationships can stifle personal growth as well. The development of adult individuals stops if one's sense of self becomes subordinate. It takes two emotionally healthy, interdependent people to build a happy marriage. Good relationships have few secrets, lots of give and take, plus uninhibited intellectual, spiritual and physical intercourse.

UMEWE
You, me and a process called we,
Alone or together can be joyously free;
When I work to grow me,
Respect and support you,
And let God decide
 If the reverse will be true.

"The process of getting good information from others starts with assuming that you don't know and that the other person will add something of value." Art

Humans resist change because learning screws up the comfort and security of knowing.

LEARNING SCREWS UP KNOWING

The chain of command, our traditional method of organizing people for work has become a cumbersome, outdated ball and chain. The system doesn't work anymore because it is based on the erroneous assumption that people at the top know best. At one time, knowledge meant power. But today, people who make decisions based on knowing are displaying a degree of insanity. They are out of touch with reality because the world is changing so fast, no single person could possibly keep up.

Who knows what occurred yesterday, last week or last month that will impact our endeavors tomorrow? For example, a retailer might be aware that an item sold well last month and feel secure in reordering more. But a less expensive, higher quality product could already be moving through the distribution channel, introducing the prospect of excess inventory and lost sales.

On the home front, you may think you know all there is to know about your spouse and children, but think again. Will they experience anything today that could alter their feelings, attitudes or perspective? To lead effectively in business, the community or as a parent at home, you must make a 180 degree mindset change to match the pace of a rapidly changing world.

Give up the facade of pretending you know and proudly declare, "I HAVEN'T GOT A CLUE!" You won't get much respect however, if you leave yourself in that position. Your next step must be to fill the knowledge gap with a method or process for finding out and taking action faster than the competition. Having a personal system of discovery, learning and doing is more important than knowing. In other words, understanding how to get information is more important than memorizing information and facts that will probably be outdated before you can make use of them.

"Communicating is difficult because it takes time to do it well and there doesn't seem to be much of it available these days." Art

COMMUNICATING PERSON TO PERSON

The close proximity of people, amplified by an expanding array of communication tools such as mobile telephones, talk radio, multi channel television and now the internet, doesn't necessarily mean we are getting closer to each other. In fact the tools themselves may be keeping us apart.

It is difficult to hear what others are trying to say in what has become a very noisy world. To protect ourselves from noise saturation, we subconsciously screen out repetitive sounds considered non-essential. More than passively letting sound waves bounce off an ear drum, really listening necessitates taking the initiative to understand what others are trying to say. Intimacy requires mutual respect and an essential element of demonstrating respect is letting others know that you are really paying attention when they speak.

To listen effectively give the sender your undivided attention. Make a production out of dropping what you are doing or politely suggest a more appropriate time, when you will be capable of listening without distraction. This activity signals that you consider the other person important enough to command all, not just part of your attention. If the time is right for a discussion, turn and face the sender directly. Establish and hold eye contact. At regular intervals throughout the conversation, restate in your own words what you think he or she has been saying. For example, "you don't want to go tonight?" This process is called paraphrasing and it lets the recipient know you are listening and that you understand. Paraphrasing also provides an opportunity to identify and correct misinterpretations.

Knowing when to give feedback is an essential but oft-times neglected communication skill. A helpful rule of thumb is: "provide feedback when the other person asks for it but even then, only in the absence of an acceptable alternative." Unsolicited feedback (particularly when it is negative) can unintentionally rob people of their dignity. It will eventually damage even promising relationships.

If you must give negative feedback, select an appropriate location. Avoid public places because the spontaneous reaction of a recipient can be unpredictable.

Put things in their proper perspective by ending on a positive note such as, "just because we focused on a negative doesn't mean that your positive strengths and contributions will be forgotten."

The valuable communication tool called feedback, is deceptively dangerous. Never give it off the cuff. Weigh the pros and cons carefully and when you must proceed, avoid the following pitfalls and traps.

- Assuming third party hearsay to be true
- Breaking a confidence in the heat of the moment
- Not having specific non-judgmental evidence to support your claim.
- Letting your own stuff skew your perspective.
- Beating around the bush with irrelevant small talk
- Getting sidetracked or not sticking to the issue, problem or behavior.
- Proceeding without the recipient's full attention.

"There is an important relationship between planning and visioning. When one is used without the other or when the two are inappropriately melded, performance suffers." Art

"The best laid plans of mice and men…" The skepticism of Robert Burns about the usefulness of planning is justified because in a rapidly changing world, events seldom unfold the way we predict. Yet businesses, families and individuals continue to use conventional long range planning.

BE A PIRATE OR JOIN THE NAVY

I was living on the prairies when North America experienced its first energy crisis. Industry and government planners had been projecting the continued escalation of price when the bottom suddenly fell out of the oil market. I watched all manner of long range plans fly from board room windows- followed closely by their stunned authors.

I learned from that experience that long range planning is at best a waste of time and at worst dangerous. Visioning has become a critical factor in creating plans that work. Planning is like joining the navy, it involves serious control issues that demand commitment and high levels of performance. Visioning by contrast, feels more like being a pirate because it focuses on creativity and energy. The odds of success increase when your process uses both. Visioning engages the wonder, creativity and flexibility of the child that still resides within you (albeit buried under layers of shoulds and how tos). Planning applies the analytical skill and structural discipline of a trained mind.

Here's how they work together:

Imagine yourself in an open field wanting to reach a distant mountain range. The child within you sees the mountains as magical and mysterious. To the pragmatic adult part of you, the mountains appear a long way off and formidable. You look through a set of binoculars and notice a clump of trees five miles away but in the general direction of the mountains. Because the trees are close, you notice the pitfalls and traps between you and the first objective. Your concern diminishes because there will be no surprises. With good data you can plan effectively and overcome the obstacles. You execute your move towards the trees with enthusiasm because you are proceeding in the general direction of those wondrous mountains, while at the same time you are confident that the trees represent a realistic short term goal. Note that the navy and the pirate parts of you are fully involved.

Once the trees are reached, your child once again stares longingly at the mountains while the adult refocuses the binoculars to accommodate your position change. Obstacles beyond your initial scope are now in plain view and you can plan stage 2.

Visioning steers towards a possibility, creating the pirate's will to win and desire to belong; while planning makes a commitment to reach a specific step along the way and enforces navy discipline and control.

"If I ever plan to move towards a beautiful mountain range, I'll take my faithful companion along with me as well as the binoculars." Art

ALL I NEED TO KNOW ABOUT FRIENDSHIP

-I learned from my dog

Attending to the needs of a dog is a tough assignment but the compensation for doing so is excellent. Why are K9s considered man's best friend when dog ownership means cleaning up messes, guarding against pests and parasites, feedings, vacuuming unsightly fur balls and forced marches in bad weather? Let's take a look at what a dog/person relationship can teach us about friendships in general. Dogs and friends:

- Inject productive ritual into our lives: The caring routine keeps us "out there," experiencing life. Being there for or with a 4 legged friend opens the door to serendipity. For example, if you weren't out walking the dog, you might not have noticed the beautiful sunset or met that charming new neighbor.
- Offer unconditional affection and support: Being alone reduces the survival chances for most of God's creatures. Animals in their natural habitats band together in practical configurations influenced by instinct. The bonding at times resembles affection-the life blood of friendship.
- Remind us to care for self and others: Pets stimulate reflection and meditation. Spiritual presence makes people more responsive to their own needs and the needs of others. People often fail to recognize their own needs until they see themselves in relation to someone else.

- Keep us open and available for others: People must open up in order to make friends. Medical research has proven that petting an animal opens the cardiovascular system and reduces blood pressure. Dog people are typically open to accepting and giving affection. (Pit bull owners may be an exception.)
- Challenge us when we fail to act: A dog and a good friend will not sit idly by when you forget to attend to their or your own needs. They prove their friendship by confronting you without inhibition whenever the situation calls for it.

"Switching from man's best friend to man's worst nightmare; is there anybody in your life that has a personal mission to change you? Their actions say more about them than you." Art

> The insignificant behaviors of other people really gets on my nerves at times. I remember suffering bad hair days because a school chum smacked his lips while chewing his lunch.

WE HAVE SEEN THE ENEMY AND HE IS US

-Pogo

The closer people are to each other, the more powerful annoyance factors become. For example, I drive my family (all females) around the bend when I leave the toilet seat up. At our cottage, the girls painted a sign on the underside of the toilet seat. Their not so subtle reminder reads, KEEP A LID ON IT!

Overreaction to the annoying behavior of others is usually about control issues and being judgmental. Humans spend an inordinate amount of time trying to get others to do as they do, believe as they believe, feel as they feel and I am ashamed to say, even chew as they chew. We focus on the faults of others because doing so is less painful than accepting and having to deal with our own shortcomings. "I'll feel better once I fix a few people out there," is an obsession that provides little in the way of value to those doing or those being done unto.

A "stay busy fixing others" raison-d'etre, is a subconscious diversionary strategy that makes sure we will never have time to improve ourselves. Others resent people shoulding on them. Human beings universally dislike being changed (wet babies excluded).

The psychological term to "project," suggests that we notice things in others because of what is going on in ourselves. Interpersonal problems are therefore best corrected from our own side of the fence. It's amazing how quickly other people change when we adjust our own attitudes and behavior.

You can make a significant contribution towards fixing the world, by fixing yourself first.

The following story gets to the bottom line.

A father wanting to occupy his children gave them a magazine picture of the world that he had torn into small pieces. A few minutes later the children returned with the picture taped together. "How did you put it together so fast", the father inquired. The children responded, "there was a picture of a man on the back of the page. Once we put him back together the world was fixed too."

"It would take a genius to fix me,' is a defeatist's lament. Did you know that you already have personal genius sitting patiently on the side lines just waiting to jump in and help you win?" Art

THE OAK IN
THE ACORN

Most of the skills and attitudes essential to your survival were in place before you reached the age of five. Your personal coping pattern is a highly evolved and specialized combination of fight and flight predisposition. Some will succeed by confronting challenges head on. Others will achieve because they go with the flow and know how to stay out of harm's way. If there is no single best way, what is the ultimate secret to success?

Traits and interests that were evident during early childhood may be a valuable key to your success and happiness as an adult. Re engaging what turned your crank as a youngster builds on natural strengths and shuns the adult preoccupation with overcoming weakness. The ancient Greeks called this unique pattern of personal capability a daimon. The Romans referred to it as the genius. Following one's daimon or genius produces strength and wellness. By contrast, pursuit of non-compatible activities detracts. The medical term disease comes from the recognition of dis-ease within the body. Dis-ease occurs when people stray too far from their natural calling. A multi billion dollar self help industry is based on an erroneous assumption. They focus on what's wrong then offer "one size fits all" solutions to correct faults.

A colleague once said, "teach a child to use a hammer and for awhile, the whole world looks like a nail." The belief that what works for some will work for all, causes people to gullibly buy self help products (such as diet foods) that seldom produce the desired results. What doesn't work isn't the product, rather the people who buy them. 85 percent of all self help books, tapes and other items sit unused. The mere act of taking delivery of an improvement aid reduces the "need to improve" tension in most people to the extent that they no longer feel compelled to use the product. Marketers buy and sell mailing lists of people who habitually purchase self-help programs. They know that the improvement "dis-ease" is seldom cured and that obsessive desire marks a high probability of making additional sales.

A doable solution to success and happiness is to rediscover your daimon or genius, and making the most of who you are.

- Talk to parents and others who knew you as a child and rediscover the natural direction of your fancy before inhibition set in.
- Develop deep-seated talent, the germ of which is already inside you.
- Build careers, hobbies and relationships consistent with your nature.

"Doing what is best for a loved one isn't always a pleasant experience. Tough love hurts the giver." Art

> Living today is more complicated than it used to be. As a parent I know the agony of watching children leave the nest unprepared. Being unprepared is an opinion my children didn't share until they had kids of their own.

TOUGH LOVE

There are many pitfalls and traps along the way and we desperately want to protect our maturing children from making serious mistakes.

Once children reach their mid teens, you are out of the control seat. They are like arrows. You can sharpen, aim and provide thrust but once you let go of the bow string, they're on their own.

The most effective safety net for the short and longer term protection of children is a set of core values. Values come from exposure to family, friends and institutions.

But sometimes even the best parental preparation fails and a loved one engages in destructive behavior.

A support process called tough love is designed to help when all else fails. Tough love means affording people the dignity of choosing their own way; even when you believe the path they have selected to be wrong or dangerous. It is an intervention of last resort for people incapable of learning without the pain of personal experience. The most difficult part of tough love is standing back and allowing the hurting person to bear the full consequence of his or her actions.

A "let go and let God," mindset helps parents muster the courage to begin the tough love process and keep the faith once the going gets difficult. To make tough love work, the first thing you need to know about God is, "you ain't him." Avoid the natural urge to control the lives of young adults. Benefits seldom occur from interfering with the choices of others. Meddling often has the opposite effect because it encourages the struggling loved one to prolong the dysfunction, long after he or she would have stopped had they been left to their own devices.

"To bee or not to be? The honey bee has a time tested survival strategy that human beings could learn from." Art

There is a balance between explorers and dreamers who instinctively act on ideas without much planning and those who prefer to work from a blueprint. One example is the songwriter who creates and the people who make the music by following the composer's score. According to the experts, balance happens somewhere around a ratio of 85:15.

THE 85:15 SURVIVAL FACTOR

Bees have been around for centuries. Their system of survival obviously works. When a worker bee returns to the hive after a production trip, it walks a tiny triangle whose apex points directly to a proven source of pollen. The hive's majority is predisposed to pick up on these signals and fly directly to the advertised bonanza. That's where the term beeline comes from.

While the dancing worker bees are wiggling their bottoms, they also emit audible bleeps. The interval between these sounds pinpoints the exact distance to a pollen source. Using this excellent navigation system, bees can land on the head of a pin several miles away.

The bee's signal/response mechanism is marvelous, but the main reason for the longevity of this industrious species is that only 82 percent of the hive is capable of interpreting the pollen song and dance. The other 18 percent are mutants who are genetically incapable of following directions. This screwed up minority flies off with no idea of where they are going. Most return empty handed but a few accidentally bump into a new pollen supply. Without the proper ratio of mutants, bees would soon deplete all of the known sources of pollen and the hive would disappear. If man were to create life he would probably make a fatal mistake. He would manufacture a perfect life, which in reality is the greatest imperfection of all. Perfect systems kill because they eventually deplete available resources.

Parents and teachers have good intentions when they create standards and rules for children. They make a huge mistake however, when they insist on applying the rules across the board. That peculiar child with the apparent discipline problem could be exhibiting the natural behaviors of a mutant explorer from the 18 percentile. Like the notoriously ill mannered and poor student Winston Churchill, some trouble makers are destined to break with tradition and find ways of making our world a better place.

"The valuable lesson from bees is the necessity of accurately interpreting the signals of others. Knowing how to send messages so that hive mates understand is essential to human survival." Art

From the moment of birth humans have an insatiable appetite for recognition. As herding creatures we are programmed to support and be supported by one another. The primal instinct to belong and be valued is so powerful, that fear of rejection causes intense mental and physical trauma.

GIVING POSITIVE FEEDBACK

Your evolution as a group member began with your mother. It quickly grew to include family, friends then on to an ever changing collection of communities such as schools, neighborhoods, church groups, political parties, and sport teams.

To remain effective and healthy every group member needs to receive signals that they are appreciated. Positive feedback is preferable but ignored people will lash out with destructive behavior to get attention, even if the attention is a kick in the pants. A sad reality is that most humans will choose bad treatment over no treatment at all. Many people are stuck in abusive relationships because they fear the unknown of "not belonging" more than the abuse they know. Community safe houses and a strong support system are essential because many victims of abuse are incapable of breaking away on their own.

Along with safety, food and affectionate touching from a caring human being, positive feedback is an essential contributor to human wellness. My experience has been that few people perform this skill well. Powerful executives were routinely shocked to learn that they were deficient in giving positive recognition. A prominent political leader commented after one of my training sessions, "if you told me yesterday that I have a problem giving positive recognition I would not have listened. But after today's practice session, I'm a believer. I resisted giving feedback because I was afraid recipients would slack off or ask for a raise. I also felt like a fake because I knew I'd inevitably have to chastise recipients for something. I was also afraid I'd leave a deserving person out-so I avoided giving recognition to anybody."

Closer to home, I held back giving my children as much positive recognition as they deserved because I erroneously assumed it would cause them to slack off. How wrong I was. On corporate morale surveys, the #1 complaint is "I don't get enough recognition."

Use the following three-step process to improve your effectiveness at providing positive recognition:

Step #1   Be specific about what has been noticed. Never use generalities such as. "You're the greatest." Rather, say something specific like, "I noticed that you picked up your toys last night without being asked."

Step #2   Let the recipient know exactly why you appreciate what has been noticed. For example, "I really appreciate what you've done because it will give us more time to read a bedtime story and your toys won't get stepped on."

Step #3   Advise the recipient that you would appreciate additional helpful contributions. Say something like, "when you help me by picking up your toys, you're making our home a better place to live and that's really important. If you can you think of other ways of helping, I'd really appreciate it."

"In this day and age it is difficult to have a pioneering experience. I unwittingly set one up for my family." Art

CAMPING OUT

The Mrs. Herself and I enjoyed camping until we qualified for a seniors discount at a national hotel chain. Similar to most forms of recreation, equipment needs evolve, i.e. become more complex and expensive as the campers mature. It took us less than a year to outgrow an intimate pup tent. Double wide, adjoining sleeping bags gave way to separate canvas cots as the passion of youth was overtaken by a shared preference for a good night's sleep. The change in sleeping arrangements was timely because during a camping trip to Louisiana, a wilderness guide had qualified me as an honorary 'open fire' chef, specializing in Cajun baked beans. Back in the 'pre Beano' days it would have been an affront to southern gentility to ask The Mrs. Herself to share an airtight sleeping bag with me. Prior to stepping up to the camper class, our last tent was a cavernous relic that looked like Barnum and Bailey surplus. We could have used three rings to accommodate our family circus. One memorable long weekend saw friends join us at the lake. It was the busiest time of the year so two women, four kids, 2 dogs and a cat, traveled early to beat the traffic and claim the best campsites. My buddy and I drove up after work.

Wanting to make life easier for their exhausted commuters, our ladies had graciously erected the tents in the middle of a secluded meadow. "Water-view is usually more expensive but we got a deal on these sites," my friend's wife exclaimed proudly. We eventually discovered that they had set up camp in a combination overflow area/drainage run off.

During the first night our 4 year-old piddled in her sleeping bag because she was terrified of bum monsters hiding in the outhouses. This insight was a gift from my friend's son. After ejecting the soiled sleeping bag, making a pajama change and standing guard with a flashlight inside a cramped outhouse, I escorted my daughter to our friend's tent and told her to crawl in beside the culprit with a penchant for scaring girls.

My act of aggression (campsite road rage) escalated the dissention on both sides. Torrential rain, thunder and lightning was next on this memorable evening's agenda. Our friend's dog went berserk after each thunder-clap. In retaliation for dropping off my daughter, the dog was slipped (still howling) under our tent flap. I awoke with a wet, shivering beagle sprawled across my face. That night we experienced what weather people call a 50 year storm. Running water at our bargain priced campsite floated a canoe, cooler and one fully loaded picnic table into the lake.

When travelling my wife and I often reflect on the memorable times we experienced as campers. The conversation takes place after room service has delivered the evening meal and housekeeping has turned down our bed.

"Polls collect information from the masses. The data is used by political decision makers to chart the nation's course. It's like driving a twisting road at break neck speed, and trying to navigate by looking in the rear view mirror." Art

One of the pleasures of aging is to reclaim the courage to be ourselves. 2 year-olds are called terrible because they aren't afraid to do it when it feels good and tell it like it is. By contrast, adults get tangled in their knickers trying to be politically correct. Civility has always meant responding appropriately within well-defined societal boundaries. Today, appropriate is defined by them (whoever they are.)

DUMBING DOWN

Politicians spend a great deal of time and your money trying to second guess what "them" wants, feels, thinks, would put up with and be willing to pay for. Polls act like a powerful anti-biotic, destroying every germ of leadership that tries to invade our political system.

Those who are influenced by polls fail to take into account that the collected data reflects the hopes, fears and attitudes of many naïve and hopelessly misguided people. A sizable chunk of respondents are non-discerning couch potatoes, drawing their every conclusion from carefully scripted media events. TV and tabloid entertainment is presented under the guise of news. After important public debates the television media assembles pundits to tell "them" what they just saw, heard and felt. Because the media has an underlying agenda to manufacture ratings, they "spin" towards sensationalism rather than truth or clarity. TV's increasing influence over what "them" hears and sees is unchallenged. The media is conditioning "them" to spectate rather than participate and they are dumbing us down in the process.

News and information today, is selected and presented for entertainment value alone. Complex issues are routinely reduced to their lowest common denominator. "Them" expects an instant and painless resolution to each and every problem. It didn't take terrorists or politicians long to discover that effective warfare must be fought during prime time. If the polls shows "them" as being unhappy with the way things are, a media event is created to shake things up. It doesn't matter to the media what the audience feels as long as it feels passionately. Depicting and even creating violence has become a productive strategy because it produces ratings and pushes competing stories off center stage. As evidenced during the OJ trial, and Clinton's Lewinski ordeal, "them" likes to buzz around gruesome or tacky stories like moths to a flame. Living vicariously through a TV set is about as productive as a dog chasing it's own tail - engaged in busy work that is going nowhere. "Them" is sitting in an unventilated room with a media engine at full throttle and getting stoned on the exhaust fumes.

The first step in substituting "them" for you and me occurred when the media discovered it could fan our psychotic search for the legendary fountain of youth. Agelessness has become a national obsession. Youth is a natural media darling because it is photogenic, less discerning than maturity and growth oriented. Keeping up youthful appearance and attitudes keeps the economy going and the sponsors happy. But it also inhibits "them" from growing up and accepting adult responsibility.

Phase two of the dumbing down process is well underway. It is no longer sufficient to simply maintain a youthful appearance. The media is setting a standard that makes it OK for "them' to act like children well into their 50's. Short attention spans, a juvenile expectation that life must be entertaining and that all problems can be resolved quickly without personal inconvenience; is preventing our poll driven political system from dealing with complex matters until the issue becomes an emergency worthy of prime time coverage.

"The opposite of collaboration is to impose on others. To establish a respect for authority in their children, parents must use personal power to enforce family rules. Once trust and respect is learned, collaboration and democracy are possible." Art

DEMOCRACY MUST START AT HOME

Violence, remains the dispute settlement tool of choice in many parts of the world. Trying to understand the use and abuse of power has captured the attention of thinkers since the beginning of time.

The Western world continues to embrace personal freedom but a growing segment of society shuns freedom's essential flip side, the need to accept personal responsibility. Many want democratic privilege without having to exhort or succumb to authority. In other words, they prefer being taken care of, rather than becoming masters of their own destiny. Our current ambivalence towards politics is a case in point. Everybody complains but few are willing to involve themselves in the democratic process.

Accepting personal authority is an essential part of civilized society. The signing of the Magna Carta marked a turning point. Absolute authority was taken from the ruling class and assigned to the masses. From then on, personal rights and freedoms have been protected by documents (constitutions) outlining rules for the deployment of power.

Without personal responsibility, even the most honorable constitutional declaration is worth no more than the paper it is written on. A democracy must operate from a fundamental set of core values and the personal willingness of its majority to defend those values at all cost.

In our democracy authority is granted to appointed individuals charged with acting on the public's behalf. But if "we the people," fail to use the democratic process to remind public servants that they serve at our leisure, a privileged aristocracy will rise to the top and assume control. These fat cats will satisfy their own needs at public expense. (Does this sound familiar?) The alternative to violence is democracy and democracy demands the acceptance and execution of personal responsibility.

Democratic principles are best taught at home. Parents need to exercise power by assuming control while their children are small. At this stage, values must be instilled or society will pay a high price. Parents must also prepare young adults to assume constantly increasing levels of personal responsibility. If values are not enforced and if privilege is not accompanied by responsibility, the democratic transfer of power will be replaced by adolescent rebellion that can last a lifetime.

"When discussions deteriorate to opinions about male vs. female superiority, I find myself defending a moderately traditional perspective. Gender predisposition in the opinion of your humble servant, is in the genes. Viva la difference"
Art

"The only difference between grown men and boys is the size, price and speed of their toys". "Sugar spice and everything nice." Old sayings supported by new research.

VALUING THE GENDER GAP

Experts are returning to the previously held view that genetics create the gender gap. Professional opinion has finally caught up to what a majority of thinking human beings have known since Adam took it in the ribs for Eve. There are significant and socially imperative differences between the behavioral predisposition of men and women.

Differences in TV habits:

When women stare into a TV set, (the information age equivalent of a stone-age campfire) they have the patience to wait while a good plot unfolds. They accept the fact that feelings are best when savored. Men adopt a hunting mindset around the living room campfire. By instinct they are obsessive about holding the family spear (remote control). Men enjoy hunting through TV channels for game(s). They prefer a quick kill (getting the score) then moving on to other game(s). The nomadic behavior of male hunters drove prehistoric women around the bend. The inherited characteristics of modern man affects today's women much the same way.

Differences in tool preference:

Power, size, speed, and noise form the cornerstone of male decision making when it comes to selecting a tool. It boggles the mind of most females to understand the attraction of a monster truck rally. Adolescent girls have been known to fake interest in macho events to connect with their less socially evolved counterparts. The process of purchasing a vehicle is an excellent example of gender preference. Women look for efficiency, quality, safety, color and comfort. Men want speed, good handling characteristics and power. The buying criteria of men more closely aligns with women as the male matures (except for a brief period during the mid life crisis when testosterone driven behavior surfaces for one last hurrah.)

Differences in the display of affection:

The Chinese concept of Yin/Yang offers ancient tips about living together. Tradition dictates that the Yang (male) should be respected for being firm, powerful and aggressive. The Yin (female) should be honored for her softness, flexibility and capacity to nurture. The graphic symbol of yin/yang suggests that the primary strength of each sex is an inherent part of the other. Ancient Chinese philosophers encouraged couples to value their differences while at the same time recognizing the capacity and necessity of compromising when the situation calls for it.

Gail Sheehy's book Passages, presents a captivating model called the "sexual diamond." It suggests that humans start out together. At puberty the male begins moving towards independence and material gain, while women are attracted to nurturing activity and spiritual development. The gap widens until age 40 (prime season for the male mid life crisis). At this point, Sheehy suggests that the two sexes are furthest apart. After 40 men become more nurturing and spiritually focused while women crave independence and goal pursuance. The good news is that the sexes meet with full compatibly once again, somewhere around the age of 65.

"An orchestra conductor once told me to focus on starting and ending together. He implied that what happens in between is less important." Art

> Nothing can begin anew, without first letting go of the old. Newborns leave the womb to begin life. Childhood fantasy is replaced by adolescent experimentation. Adults mellow as passion meets responsibility. The stability of mid life can give way to uncertainty.

ENDINGS AND BEGINNINGS

Living things either grow or they rot. Yet we often stubbornly cling to the status quo, investing a great deal of energy resisting change. It is a misleading and dangerous illusion to believe that anything can stay the same.

Why is it so difficult to let go of stuff, attitudes, habits and people? A possible answer is that our culture gives short shift to "rites of passage." For example, Australian aboriginals do not annually celebrate the day of their physical birth. Rather, they celebrate a birthday each time something of significance is learned or experienced. Every change means that a member of the community has been reborn and others share in the excitement and rejoice with each transition. Moving on is considered a happy and essential fact of life.

North Americans spend fortunes on lotions, dyes and cosmetic surgery; trying to retard the aging process. Unfortunately, this type of hanging-on inhibits growth and retards one's capacity to enjoy the unique experiences that are offered by each stage of life.

When the Romans invaded Britain, Caesar wanted assurance that his soldiers were committed to the conquest. The troops were marshaled on the beach to watch as their boats were burned-there would be no going back. The benefit of letting go is that you are making an irrevocable commitment to move forward. "Rites of passage" ceremony helps the individual by offering communal support and honoring the inherent value of change. Any group or family that does not celebrate the significant life events of its members, unwittingly fosters resistance to change.

"I don't feel any older, but I notice there are more younger people around than there used to be." Art

LATEAGERS

In a rapidly changing world, planning for the golden years is difficult. A primary challenge, is knowing when to let go. A close second is making appropriate choices to fill the vacated space. As living creatures we are destined to change. For the elderly however, transitions can be overwhelming.

The song sheets we are expected to sing from aren't suitable anymore. The notes and harmony in, "darling you are growing old" may be identical to the tune grandfather sang-but the timing has changed. When Mr. and Mrs. Chris Columbus said "till death do us part," they weren't looking at 60 years plus. Living the last half of life according to established societal scripts is like trying to waltz to a polka. The tempo of life has increased and songs are lasting much longer.

According to sociologist Gail Sheehey, the average human at 50 years of age has as much productive life ahead of them as a 21 year old living in 1901. Each human is unique and variables such as exercise, stress and nutrition have an influence, but the largest determinant of longevity is heredity. A big chunk of a person's destiny is hard wired into genes handed down from generation to generation. But we are also evolving as a species. Actuarial statistics predict that you and I will live longer than our parents. So it doesn't make any sense to use retirement models established by previous generations.

It is appropriate for today's lateager, (persons beyond 60 years of age) to go back to school, start another career, form new relationships or take up athletic endeavors such as tennis, golfing or lawn bowling. Mother Nature presents lateagers with two choices- to continually reinvent themselves and remain an active participant in life or to shrink into passivity as a spectator.

Research proves that doers fare better than spectators in terms of maintaining their health and happiness. Retirement is a dirty word when it emphasizes endings. As a living organism our focus should always be on beginnings. In his infinite wisdom, God is granting many of us additional time. It is up to us to make use of the opportunity

"Giving up a habit (even a bad one) is like losing an old friend." Art

Many habitual behaviors are a necessity. Think back to your first driving experience. Do you remember doubting that you would ever master what seemed like hundreds of disjointed tasks? I recall watching in awe as experienced drivers drove with unconscious precision.

BREAKING UP (HABITS) IS HARD TO DO

How did they know when to turn the steering wheel? They weren't even aware of the critical adjustments being made every few seconds. Habits make our lives less complicated by providing an auto pilot to accommodate repetitive activity.

Breaking a habit is difficult because in essence, you are saying goodbye to an old friend. For good or bad, the behavior you are trying to give up has been an important part of your life. And habits won't let go without a fight. If a smoker takes 25 puffs on each cigarette and smokes 25 cigarettes a day that means 625 subconscious movements of the hand. The same number holds true for the lips. It is twice that number of movements for the lungs because they inhale and exhale each puff. That adds up to a total of 2500 repetitions each and every day. For a 20-year smoker, the habit involves 18,250,000 movements. Is it any wonder people complain about not knowing what to do with their hands when they initially quit smoking?

The following three-step process, is designed to reset your auto pilot and help you shake an unwanted habit:

Imagining: The subconscious mind doesn't know the difference between thinking and reality. It takes 21 days of repeated imagining to fool the mind into believing that a mental picture is real.

Begin your quest by imagining yourself as an established success. At this point, you continue using the unwanted habit.

For example, if you want to become a non-smoker; close your eyes for 5 minutes, twice a day over a period of at least 21 days and picture yourself as the non-smoker you expect to become. Imagine benefits like the fresh and clean aroma of your clothes. Rejoice as your long lost sense of smell reacquaints you with the beautiful fragrance of a flower. You might dream about your food tasting better or notice that your complexion has improved. Proudly watch as you mentally run up several flights of stairs without wheezing. In your mind's eye, smile at a smoking buddy when he offers you a cigarette and you say, "no thanks, I'm a nonsmoker."

Conditioning: After a minimum of 21 days, the next step is to establish a "cold turkey" stop date at least one month away. Mark your STOP date on the calendar. Begin a diary and record the time and place of each cigarette smoked from here on. In your diary, rate each smoking session as high, medium or a low in terms of satisfaction. Discard spent butts into a large container with an airtight lid (a restaurant size pickle jar works).

These activities move your unwanted habit from auto-pilot to full consciousness. You create a vacuum in your subconscious mind, then during twice-daily imaging sessions, quietly fill the vacated space with positive reinforcement.

Reinforcement: On and after your targeted STOP day, symbolically throw away your habit. Each time a desire to engage in the unwanted behavior is noticed, reach for the butt jar. Close your eyes and inhale through your nose. Note the obnoxious smell. While engaging in this unpleasant activity, create a horribly unpleasant picture in your mind. When I quit smoking, I imagined a package of cigarettes that had been vomited on (not a pretty picture but it works). After a few practice sessions I could actually make myself gag. Negative stimulation weakens the impact of dangerous flashbacks that can trigger a renewal of the unwanted habit.

This habit busting process gets your subconscious mind working for rather than against you by including both positive and negative imagining.

"A difficult habit to break is keeping yourself so busy that you miss life's little pleasures." Art

THE CREATIVITY CONTINUUM

The psychoanalyst Sigmund Freud, assumed that the primary drive of mankind was to experience pleasure and avoid pain. Pleasure is the direct result of a chemical process brought on by endorphins automatically released each time the body finds a way of relieving tension. Food eases a tension called hunger. Endorphins create a pleasurable experience associated with eating. Pleasure is nature's way of encouraging the repetition of specific behaviors.

Victor Frankle thought differently. His observations of fellow prisoners in a Nazi concentration camp caused him to declare that "purpose" was man's primary reason for being. He noticed that inmates who felt they had no reason to live, just gave up and died.

People who attach no meaning to their existence, drift through life as a creature of habit, mindlessly filling then voiding their mind and body. Others become addicted to chemical highs brought on by drugs or adrenaline rushes. Seeking instant gratification, they develop insatiable appetites and require ever increasing quantities, speed, power and variety to sustain pleasure. But yesterday's rush is never enough and like Elvis, Marilyn Monroe or John Belushi, many burn out and die.

Frankel's assertion (purpose being mankind's primary reason for being), can be validated by watching people build things. They are alert and involved. The energy level of arts and craft groups is typically high because members literally live to participate in the creative process. Creativity comes from somewhere between one's imagination and his/her ability to produce. For example, a small boy visiting Michel Angelo is said to have asked the great artist how he knew that David was buried in the original block of marble. What started as Angelo's exclusive vision, was actually created by the arduous task of removing every piece of stone that didn't look like the creator's mental picture of David.

When humans are centered, they inhabit a creative space between imagination at one end of the "creativity continuum," and production (the capacity to transform vision into reality) at the other end. People will experience spiritual numbing however, if they take up permanent residence at either end of this continuum. At the visioning extreme, they become chronic daydreamers who can see possibilities but are incapable of doing anything except talk about it. At the other end, people will relegate themselves to the mindless treadmill of repetitive activity. Balancing one's self between imagination and production is the essence of creation and successful living. What Victor Frankel called meaning, happens when people create.

"Risk taking is easy when you're on familiar ground. Engaging the unknown takes courage." Art

Last on my to-do list was an innocuous trip to the barbershop. These biweekly visits usually remind me of a Norman Rockwell painting. Once in the chair, the fine art of small talk kicks in and my trials and tribulations go on hold for a soothing half-hour. Recently however, the tranquility of this retreat was shattered. Bob the barber lulled me into a false sense of security, then took advantage of me.

BREAKING A LEG

His con began with an off-hand comment about the power of what he called my "baritone voice". Because of my laid back state, I took his bait like an old bass. "I practice voice inflexion and proper breathing because on the speaker's circuit, strong pipes are an asset," I mused sleepily. "Do you sing?" The hook was set when I responded to Bob's question in the affirmative. I sighed and slipped into what I now believe was a purposely-induced hypnotic trance. I was jolted back to reality with a spin of Bob's chair, his customary signal that time was up. He dusted clipped hair off my shoulders and said, "I'll call you with details tomorrow." I erroneously assumed he was referring to my next appointment. The appointment Bob was arranging for me, was to audition for a musical being staged by a local performing arts group.

Bob obviously conditioned me with a post-hypnotic suggestion not to decline. Sunday night found me standing in front of a panel of judges. "Where is your accompaniment?" an authoritative voice boomed from dark shadows at the back of the room. I was standing on a flood lit stage, frozen like a deer caught in car headlights. "Bob didn't tell me I needed support, but I'll stomp my feet if you like?" "What's your range?" the director barked. I bit my lip to avoid saying General Electric (the only range I know). After a long silence a female voice broke the silence. "OK Art, go ahead and sing accappella." "I'm not familiar with Accappella-but I can sing Some Enchanted Evening." Unexpectedly, my response brought the house down. (I hate it when people have to explain jokes to me).

I performed my morning shower rendition of the aforementioned show tune. Without running water and the echo chamber properties of wrap around tile, I failed to create sounds that Tennessee Ernie Ford would think well of. My song ended on a high note but the auditioning experience did not. The next faux pas I'll couch in jeopardy talk because the memory is too painful to recall. "Not according to my wife. What is… can you dance?"

"You expect me to dance in a chorus line?" The troop's choreographer came on stage, took my hand and with an encouraging demeanor similar to what I used when teaching our children to walk, asked me to count to eight and distinguish between my right and left foot. "Congratulations Art," boomed the director, "you'll be appearing in our next production." I have three months to practice. The director assures me he will have a potted palm standing by for me to hide behind if the troop's coaching fails. I learned why they call performing art patrons long-haired. I'll not return to Barber Bob's until this performance is over.

"Noah saved two of everything because nature places a high value on pairs." Art

During my teenage years I was reminded regularly by friends and family that I was not living up to my full potential. They told me to bear down and work harder. In the vernacular, I was told to "pull up my socks." The following are lessons from the sock drawer.

LESSONS FROM THE SOCK DRAWER

One day it was drawn to my attention that I had erroneously donned one brown and one red sock. The laughter of colleagues was silenced with my retort, "I have an identical pair at home." No matter how different or alienated you feel, created in God's own likeness, you are part of a perfectly matched set.

- Socks need each other to do good work:
  Single socks are ideal for people with one foot but leave normal folks feeling unfulfilled. Individuals, like single socks, are incomplete units of society. It's what goes on between people, that keeps us productive and interesting.
- Dirty socks create olfactory problems:
  Humans are prone to duck a dirty job. There will always be a cleaner/fresher assignment available to keep us busy and ease our troubled conscience. But unattended dirty tasks (like grungy socks) breed undesirable beasties that can stink up your life. Create the equivalent of a weekly washday to attack that undesirable job pile. Mondays worked for our mothers.
- Never throw an odd sock out:
  My socks take separate vacations. Everything can be going well when without warning, one of them will just up and disappear. Not once has a missing sock revealed the whereabouts of its secret retreat. The rejected partner comes out of the wash clean

but can't get the job done alone. I used to throw the loners away until I discovered that partners frequently return. When loved ones disappear emotionally, don't assume the worst. It may be they simply need a time out. Wait patiently in your equivalent of an odd sock basket and odds are, your partner will return.

- Don't put stretch socks in the dryer:
  After a close encounter of the sweaty kind and a turbulent washing to eliminate dirt and grime, socks (particularly those of the high strung variety) need time to dry. Stretch socks lose elasticity when exposed to the high heat of an automatic dryer. After an emotional trauma, people (the most stretching of all God's creatures) shouldn't expect a quick recovery. Nature, given fresh air, time and space, knows how to heal.

"Sometimes it is difficult to hear what we are trying to tell ourselves. The greatest teacher the world has ever known used the following process to help people get the message." Art

GESTALT

-a valuable tool
for making tough decisions

Everybody likes a good joke. But what is it that actually makes us laugh? According to experts the magic formula is a vivid mental picture of the absurd appearing suddenly and quite different from what we had anticipated. Have you ever tried to explain a punch line when somebody didn't get it? Repeating a joke never works because there is no power without timing and surprise.

An effective form of problem solving called Gestalt Therapy operates on the same principle. The descriptive German word Gestalt means to instantly grasp a sense of the whole. A similar English expression is the familiar "ah hah" used when a blinding flash of the obvious helps us get the picture. Like a well delivered joke, the Gestalt process disarms your defense mechanism. It can open the door to understanding personal issues and help you create workable solutions. Fritz Pearls is reputed to be the world's first Gestalt Therapist but the parables of Jesus used the same technique.

I became my own Gestalt Therapist when I faced a difficult career choice that necessitated moving my family. This move would be a radical change for us. I arranged two chairs so that they faced each other and read the parable of the old wineskin and the new wine. (Mathew 9:17) Old wine skins have no give to them while it is the nature of new wine to grow and expand. My process began in earnest when I sat in one of the chairs and assumed the role of an old wineskin.

First I recounted the security and comfort of my current situation, expressing affection for my history. I changed chairs and assumed the identity of a new wine. My pulse quickened at the images of exciting challenges, different people and new places. After this rush I changed chairs again and asked the old wineskin if there was anything it wanted to say to the new wine. A scathing indictment of being irrational, thoughtless and inconsiderate followed. After the outpouring, I changed chairs and asked the new wine how it felt about what had just been said. With equal passion, accusations of being a habitual bum dragger and missing opportunities because of inappropriate fear rained down on the empty chair.

Additional questions were asked of both participants. "What parts of the other's position frightens you most?" "What would you accept if you had to?" "How will you survive if the decision doesn't go your way?" After a number of exchanges both chairs experienced a long silence. There was nothing left to say. Finally, my chest heaved a giant sigh and I blurted, "I guess what I'm trying to tell myself is...." And the decision emerged, complete with a plan that took both sides of the argument into account.

If you find it difficult to work the Gestalt process alone, use a trusted friend to ask the questions or engage the services of a professional therapist.

"You can't grow until you throw. Old ideas and outdated ways of doing things must die before new possibilities can emerge. It's not always easy to let go." Art

Before we can learn anything, we must first unlearn (let go of previously held assumptions). Unlearning is a form of death. Throughout our lives, humans must die many times in order to grow.

IS LEARNING WORTH DYING FOR

One of our more traumatic life transitions involves going through the "terrible 2" stage, not as the parent, tough as that exposure may be, but as a child experiencing the development of consciousness. Until the age of 2, people feel omnipotent. Children assume they are the center of the universe and expect the world to respond to their every whim. What a shock when Mom and Dad start laying down the rules and introduce the concept of consequence. This parental responsibility is akin to a mother bird kicking baby birds out of the nest. Every child must in a sense die before he or she can successfully evolve to the next stage of life. The story of Adam and Eve's banishment from the Garden of Eden is a Biblical account of the pain associated with the development of consciousness.

Unlearning is unpleasant because like the process of dying, learning involves letting go of cherished attitudes, habits, people, places and beliefs. Elizabeth Kubler Ross in her insightful books on the death experience, identifies emotional stages that humans go through. Her research suggests that people experience:

• denial (it can't be happening to me).
• anger (at doctors, friends, family and God).
• bargaining (maybe if I try harder and become a better person I will survive).
• depression (recognition that the jig is up).

- acceptance (time to tie up loose ends and say goodbye).

Disruptive behavior is often a precursor to success. Like the terminally ill who have already worked through denial, people in the process of letting go of a long cherished attitude or belief get upset. Facilitators or parents, who misread the early stages of learning often intervene and try to stop what they consider dysfunctional anger. By doing so, they unwittingly retard development.

If people stick with their feelings when facing physical or intellectual death, and work through all the steps of this painful process, they enter the final stage called acceptance. Accepting the inevitability of death does not mean giving up. Acceptance provides an essential foundation of enlightenment and is fundamental to growth.

A colleague specializing in palliative care commented on the beauty and richness of experience when a patient, family and friends work the dying process successfully. Some survivors have a spiritual awakening that diminishes fear and resistance for the rest of their lives. Others, stuck in the process either prolong suffering or stuff their feelings and become bitter.

"A process worth learning, is how to plan effectively. Starting off on the right foot is a great way to begin." Art

Preparing for a planning session demands more than the collection of statistics, facts and figures. Getting a group of divergently thinking people into the right headspace, is an essential but oft-neglected first step.

SETTING THE STAGE FOR PLANNING

Rampant and unpredictable change has made it almost impossible to develop meaningful long-range plans. Agreeing to move in a general direction and establishing behavioral boundaries has become a functional alternative to detail. The following process can help individuals, families, community groups and businesses prepare for planning during turbulent times.

Step #1: Imagine then document a preferred future.

Don't be constrained by current reality, go ahead and imagine the ideal. If you are part of a group, go through the visioning process as an individual first. Have each member present a mental picture of his or her preferred future. After hearing from everybody, look for and document emerging themes. Consolidate the themes into a vision of a preferred future that a sizable majority can accept as worth moving towards.

Step #2: Clarify your core values. Reflect on fundamental beliefs at the core of your group's historical success (or lack thereof). Document these, then shift from past to the future tense. Identify beliefs that would help you move towards a shared vision of the preferred future. Document the groups future beliefs separately.

Step #3: Compare values from the past to values needed for future success:

Start with what has worked in the past and add or modify with beliefs from your future list. Consolidate your thoughts into three or four words that will catch the essence of the merged beliefs. Examples of commonly occurring core values are integrity, quality, service, trust, responsiveness, innovation and caring.

Step #4: Establish behavioral boundaries:

The three or four words you select to express your group's core values are used like suitcases to carry an ever-changing array of guidelines, rules and policies. The benefit of using suitcase words (icons if you wish) to identify your core values is the ability to update their content without causing confusion. Next, ask customers, family members, friends or group members what they would need to see more or less of to prove that you are living the identified core values. During the visioning process, dialogue is more important than agreement on details. Core values are most effective when used as an act of creation. Power is diminished when they are used as another method of control.

The visioning process I have documented, establishes direction and will help your group set behavioral boundaries. In other words, members will know where they are going and what they believe in. You are now adequately prepared to undertake short term planning. If you must (and you will) change plans to accommodate a changing situation, your team will adjust without losing heart.

"A raison d'etre (reason for being) helps people maintain enthusiasm for ongoing tasks or projects." Art

SERVICE: THE DYSFUNCTION BUSTER

According to Webster dysfunctional means impaired or abnormal. A group whose members have not established or bought into a meaningful purpose for being together are destined to become unproductive and lethargic.

Employees working for dysfunctional organizations are uninspired. They typically drag themselves out of bed each day for the paycheck, as means of getting out of the house or to secure a pension at career's end.

When a family is unclear about the purpose of their being together, parents and the children will limp through life. Only their basic survival needs will be met. People from dysfunctional families experience little in the way of joy or enthusiasm. Children leave the nest with low self-esteem and a limited expectation of what the world has to offer them. Their pessimistic attitude is always self-fulfilling. An effective way of helping a dysfunctional person, group or family, is to introduce them to a compelling reason for being. Once a meaningful purpose has been accepted, people instinctively start removing the roadblocks that inhibit success. Healthy humans are herding creatures at heart and have a strong need to belong to a group. But humans are also thinkers and must constantly remind themselves why continued membership remains beneficial. Many leaders and parents fail because they do not develop a sense of shared purpose between group members.

Most time-honored human callings are service oriented. People who believe that their output is genuinely beneficial to others, will contribute with head, heart and hands. Being of service to one's family; community, country or God has always commanded respect. Service motivates ordinary people to do extraordinary things.

How to use service as an antidote for personal or group dysfunction:

• Show the person, family or group how they can be of service to others.
• Provide information and teach the skills required to do a job well.
• Help isolated people get involved with others.
• Constantly remind members of the value (to others) of their group's output.
• Help people learn to celebrate small and large successes along the way.

"My fundamental beliefs cause me to make sense of the world in a specific and highly personal way." Art

For healthy people, life's lessons produce results. These learnings culminate and form fundamental beliefs called values. Values are valuable because they establish boundaries for personal behavior and promote successful living.

THE VALUE OF VALUES

Be it a family, business or a country, no organization can exist by rules alone. There will always be situations not covered by established policy. For example, my family lived in the far north for a time. Prior to moving there, we had a rule, "children are expected to return home when the streetlights come on". Close to the Arctic Circle during the month of June, the sun doesn't set until well after midnight. We had to change the rule.

Once upon a Bible story there was a group of people wired into a perpetual wild party. They engaged in all manner of raucous and sinful activity. A more serious member was concerned about what bad behavior was doing to his friends. Needing space to think, he left the confusion and went off by himself. When the man returned, he gathered his spaced out friends and spoke to them. "I have been to the mountain top and have some good news and some bad news. On the bright side, I have negotiated with the man upstairs. He reduced the thousands of things you shouldn't be doing, down to 10. The rowdies cheered and their attention was directed towards the stone tablets he was carrying. "The bad news is, these ten items are all-encompassing and include everything you are doing."

Like the 10 commandments, values provide an essential common denominator for behavior that can help people navigate successfully in unfamiliar territory. Teaching values early is important because everything is new territory for a child. Parents can't be there to help youngsters make the right choice every time.

Values have a future tense called vision. Vision and values are flip sides of the same coin because they link the future of individuals to key learnings from the past. The largest determinant of how people choose to behave today, is their conscious or below conscious expectation of what the future holds in store. Effective leaders (including parents), know how to use the powerful double wham-my of values and vision to help others develop the will to win and a desire to belong.

" The root word in civilization is civil. Synonyms include courteous, well behaved, respectful, refined, mannerly and polite. Our society will fail if we don't return to the basics and behave in a civilized manner. " Art

Productive communities know and understand their history. They share compatible values and expectations, work to influence what they are becoming, know how to use resources and are tolerant of each other. Communication is their lifeblood. Members develop sending and receiving skills and consistently demonstrate a willingness to go the extra mile.

COMMUNITY AND CIVILITY

Television introduced "in your face and get to the point quick, " journalism. This aggressive approach destroys community because the output is usually at the expense of, or inconsiderate towards somebody. Community demands that its members feel heard and respected. When real people have something to say, it takes time. Genuine dialogue seldom presents itself in the articulate 60 second sound bites that the media prefers.

The emergence of talk radio reflects the desire of community members to spend more time discussing and thinking about important issues. Community services such as letters to the editor and internet chat lines, are high tech transformations of the time honored town hall meeting. At town hall meetings, full expression of thought was every bit as important as the need to reach a conclusion. Good communication processes build community by getting results while at the same time, validating the importance of every member by really listening to what is being said.

The cornerstone of community is a simple yet profound concept called civility. Civil implies courteous and polite in act and speech. Civility seems a bit old fashioned because we associate it with kinder, gentler times. But civility means more than superficial politeness. A 19th century Englishman, Oliver Hereford said, "a gentleman is someone who never hurts another person's feelings unintentionally."

Today, rude and vulgar remarks are often heard on the street. People who use foul language in public are either unaware or don't care about their impact on passers by. Open displays of insensitivity alienate people from each other and eventually erodes the well being of a community. The effectiveness of a society strengthens with civil discipline, including mundane but surprisingly beneficial human interactions such as chivalry, manners and common courtesy.

"Losing the willingness to trust weakens a community because fear fills the vacuum." Art

Trust commands little attention, even though it frequently involves matters of life and death. Examples of trust include faith in the weight bearing capacity of a ladder, assuming that fellow drivers will stay in their lane or that the pharmaceutical company has tested your prescription for dangerous side effects.

TO TRUST
OR FEAR

We place our lives in the hands of unknown chemists, engineers, trades people and random passers by every day. Beginning life as one of the planet's most helpless creatures, humans are dependent on parents and other adult caregivers for an extended period of time. Civilized society could not survive without our trusting nature.

A leading psychologist Jack Gibb suggested, "trust creates flow and gentles the mind-body-spirit." The opposite happens when fear replaces trust. When fear prevails, individuals and communities regress to a primitive state of kill or be killed. Fear based conditioning begets more fear and leads to an increase in violence.

Gibb asked, "is the world dangerous? Can people be trusted? Should we try to maintain our childlike trust and help children to do so? Or should we develop caution, be appropriately wary and be realistically prepared for danger?" Danger does exist. People get mugged, women and children are subjected to violence at home, there are companies who cheat customers and our democracy includes dishonest politicians. So how do we prepare the next generation? Do we teach them to bear arms when walking in their own neighborhood? Should they be conditioned to avoid participation in our political process?

We teach our children to expect evil from strangers regardless of statistics that prove most child abuse comes from family and friends. Society cannot eliminate violence completely but it can work to contain the premise upon which it thrives. Every community must make a choice to trust or fear. By choosing the latter, communities become defensive rather than creative. They increase psychotic behavior when they exclude rather than include each other

"Keeping the faith when things seem out of control is possible if you have a trusted method of regaining your bearings after the crisis" Art

Great events are attributed to men and women who had the courage to share powerful dreams. Conversely, even the most successful people and civilizations crumbled once purpose was forgotten.

DO YOU HAVE A NORTH STAR

Collective vision is an essential part of developing a healthy culture at home, at work or out in the community. Without a reason for being (purpose), human enterprise is destined to fail.

Reason for being has been used by great leaders throughout history to help followers see the potential of a new direction. It is the future tense of values (i.e. "because we share common beliefs-look at what we are capable of.") Organizations with members who do not share core values are certain to share an uncertain future. Without common ground there is no possibility of sharing a preferred future.

Reason for being works in conjunction with, but is not actually part of the planning process. The sole purpose of a reason for being is to keep group members from becoming disoriented. It is used the same way the early explorers used the North Star. They never expected to actually reach the North Star, but they could use it to get anywhere. When they were blown off course, a navigator would take a bearing off this stable celestial marker. Once re oriented, the captain could chart a new course with confidence.

Groups and individuals who take the time to distill a reason for being, feel less threatened when their world becomes unmanageable. Faith has always played a large part in helping people survive difficult situations. Like the North Star, a reason for being will be there during and after each crisis. The "reason for being" provides a timeless, superordinate reference point that can help disoriented people get themselves back on track.

"Many churches are failing to realize their desired outcome. Flocks are dwindling in number when they could be growing. " Art

THAT OLD TIME RELIGION

Observation leads me to conclude that people with strong religious beliefs have a distinct advantage over others who choose to go it alone. Trusting in a higher power, believers appear to be in harmony with nature and better equipped at coping when events move beyond their control. This faith advantage has not gone unnoticed by the masses. The success of books such as A Course in Miracles, The Celestine Prophecy and Care of the Soul, indicate that increasing numbers of people are expressing a renewed interest in spirituality. Yet many churches sit half empty. Comparing religious expression to the process of making music provides a possible answer.

People trying to master a musical instrument take part in a relentless ritual called scale practice. Listening to a beginner do scales is akin to finger nails scratching on a chalk board. Effective music teachers differentiate themselves by finding creative ways to help beginners maintain their love of music. During the vulnerable initial phase of development (when scale work is essential) they employ creative ways of making practice more enjoyable.

Accomplished musicians understand that repetition develops technique and that good technique is the foundation of great music. Even the masters hone their talent by practicing scales. A great virtuoso once said; "if I miss a day of practice I know it, two days and my wife knows it, but when I miss three days the whole world knows."

Musicians from all sections of the orchestra, practice scales to develop personal technique. But they understand that more than technique must be delivered to gain respect from the outside world. Most religious people pray and study the Bible. But growing congregations do more than pray and study. Like the effective music teacher's use of scale practice, successful church leaders use prayer and the Word as tools to help their members contribute in the outside world. Just as budding musicians are lost when scale practice is the primary focus, the church is losing potential members by not highlighting their music - the ability to do good work.

> At the watershed of midlife, people must either accept living within the "box" they have spent the first half of their lives building or choose a path of continued growth.

GREEN YOU GROW, RIPE YOU ROT

Staying with a comfortable routine is tempting because on the surface stable lifestyles offer security (a predictable and non-threatening repeat of past experience). The problem with this option is that fixed existence is an illusion. Everything around and within you is constantly changing. For example, everybody will eventually lose family and friends. We are all subject to life altering injury, disease, natural disasters and manmade catastrophe. At the cellular level our body rebuilds itself every 7 years.

Choosing a comfortable pew sets you up for failure even though you may be ecstatic about the way things are. Scientists suggest that perfectly adapted creatures are susceptible to extinction because they are incapable of finding options. By contrast, people who continue experimenting with life stay alert, informed and involved. They also live longer, happier and more prosperous lives. Today's average 50 year old has as much productive life ahead of him or her as a 21 year old did at the turn of the century. If I wanted to, I could become a brain surgeon. (fat chance-the Mrs. Herself won't even let me carve a turkey). The implication of increased longevity has not yet sunk into society's collective consciousness. Many people give up on life prematurely because they missed the brass ring their first time round. They fail to comprehend that life's carousel continues to spin and fresh starts are always possible.

As long as you are alive there will be opportunity to expand your horizons and try new things.

A survival troika:

- Never close the door on your social circle. Find new ways of letting people come (and go) in your life. Keep the skill, courage and willingness to meet people alive.
- Break out of the box periodically and do something different. Don't be contained by convention. Keep pushing the envelope and experiment with life. Trying new things may just be a playful activity today but with a single stroke, destiny could make it a survival factor.
- Never let yourself become dependent on other people. Learn how to cook, do the banking, make important decisions, travel, make your own friends and pursue personal interests.

"I was told that there was nothing to dancing. Just put one foot in front of the other, keep off your partner toes, avoid collisions and pretend you are having fun" Art

DANCING IN THE DARK

I fondly remember when dancing in the dark meant romance and delightful evenings filled with sensuous anticipation. Recently all that changed for me, particularly the "in the dark" part. My problem with dancing is neither degenerative nor age related. It started the day the Mrs. Herself and I signed up for lessons. Suddenly, everything had to be done by numbers. Passion and counting in my humble opinion make strange bedfellows but I must concede that valuable insights were gained during my dance lessons.

 A non-negotiable rule of dance is that women must follow the man's lead. Peculiar, my finding the last bastion of male authority on a dance floor that I resisted like the plague for most of my life. I played in a band from the age of 14 on through to my mid 20s so I had a good excuse.

When my wife and I finally started dancing together, we chose from the only two options that were available to us at the time - R&R or the simple Texas two step for slower music. Dancing in the good old days was simple, you either gyrated wildly or polished your belt buckle.

I used to envy people who had mastered the art of ballroom dancing. Fred and Ginger look magnificent in those old romantic movies but after a few lessons, I learned the truth. Those poor sods were working their hearts out. As spectators, we saw them gazing into each other's eyes and floating gracefully. But behind the facade, they were frantically counting steps and struggling to keep out from under each other's feet. The image of ballroom dancing is golden pondish, like loons floating effortlessly on tranquil waters. Below the surface, webbed feet are paddling franticly to keep the loon's head above water.

Lessons from the dance floor:

- When the man leads with his left foot the woman must respond with her right. This validation of the Chinese Yin Yang philosophy suggests that a couple does its best work when partners behave differently.
- Move with the line of dance or get off the floor. Go against the flow and you will disrupt things by bumping into people. Synchronism demands discipline. You have a responsibility to go by the rules.
- Dancing integrates mind, body and spirit. It is one of the more enjoyable methods of keeping body and soul together.
- Rhythm is more important than melody. Move with the pulse of life and don't be distracted by less relevant factors.

After our lessons conclude, I trust that dancing will resume its natural flow. I also expect that once again it will elicit passion. The gain behind the pain of this experience is that my wife and I are moving towards a higher level of performance in dance and our married life. Putting up with the equivalent of mundane counting is essential to all beginnings. Not being afraid to make a mistake, having fun and learning from experience produces happy endings.

"Shakespeare said the whole world is a stage. People sometimes get trapped by their role in life." Art

In ancient times, actors played multiple roles by covering their face with a variety of masks called facades. Modern language adapted the word facade to mean putting on a front or false appearance.

LIVING THE FACADE

Wearing a façade can be useful at times, for example, forcing yourself to smile at a well intentioned friend when you are really disappointed. Or masking one's fear of public speaking in order to perform in front of an audience. Problems occur however, when performers forget they are playing a role and that the audience is responding to the mask they are wearing, not the person behind it. Facades that gain a high level of audience appeal can produce privilege for the wearer. But unwary recipients often pay a high price when the performance ends.

Adoring fans grant privilege and overlook shortcomings they would not accept from friends, neighbors or family. For example, John Kennedy and Bill Clinton were notorious womanizers, Woody Allen's romantic involvement with a step daughter, Elvis was addicted to drugs and prone to violent mood swings. In the extreme, O.J. Simpson was found not guilty of murder in spite of overwhelming evidence to the contrary.

It is not surprising that celebrities are frequently victimized by their own fame. Many performers grow accustomed to created fantasy and start believing press clippings depicting them as larger than life. But with time the facade fades and these disillusioned, lonely people suddenly realize there is nothing of themselves left behind the image. Many reach for chemical highs and eventually die from addiction.

Regular folks succumb to a debilitating illusion when they accept career or position as the essence of their person. Roles such as mother, husband, child or friend can smother a healthy sense of self, if taken to the extreme. For example, parents often experience an empty nest depression when it finally dawns on them that they are no longer key players in the lives of their children. Unprepared people retire from active careers and find themselves alone with no sense of purpose. Living a facade turns human beings into a human doing. And once the doing stops; there is nothing left but the echo of applause.

How to avoid being damaged by your façade:

- Maintain a variety of interests and hobbies that have nothing to do with your job.
- Spend time with real people who care about the person behind your mask.
- Let the people at work see who you really are and make them respect you as a person
- Don't let colleagues become overly dependent on you.

"Tracking the consumer's evolving perception of value, has replaced quality and customer service as the primary focus of successful business." Art

Quality was the primary objective of tradesmen prior to the industrial revolution. Because everything was hand made, only a wealthy few could afford to purchase manufactured goods. Mass production made goods and services available to the masses but quality was forced to take a back seat. Quality is making a slow but steady recovery. Consumers today expect it all- quality, low price and superb service.

TRACKING OUR EVOLVING PERCEPTION OF QUALITY

The evolution of Quality:

Phase #1 Products offer more, bigger and faster. The keyword is Production.

Long in the tooth readers will remember the day when quality meant having more stuff such as size, features, speed, chrome, colors or packaging. Ultra modern devices were advertised on TV as capable of almost anything. If Mom's Kitchen Miracle Maker couldn't do it, the world didn't need it. A quality car was big, had long tail fins, multiple colors and lots of dials, lights and knobs. Styles were changed every year and obsolescence was built in. Our perception of quality created a "throw away" society.

Phase #2 Products work to the manufacturer's standard. The keyword shifts to Quality.

A significant change occurred and at first, American auto makers did not pay any attention. German engineers introduced the Volkswagon Beetle. This car offered the exact opposite to the products of North American manufacturers. Volkswagon was selling economy and reliability. I remember sticking my head inside a bug and slamming the door to experience an ear pop. American cars were not airtight. This feature inspired a successful TV commercial in which two cars were dropped in a lake. The bug floated while the competitor sank - proof that Beatles were better built. There were no extras on a Volkswagen, so the consumer experienced fewer service problems. Our evolving definition shifted from "more" to "it works." Quality meant that a product would do what design engineers said it should do.

Phase #3 Products meet or exceeds the customer's expectation. The keyword becomes Service.

The Japanese changed the rules of the game by convincing consumers they deserved more than conformance to the manufacturer's standard. Consumers were conditioned to expect delight from the total experience. If any part of the customer experienced failed, the product was considered sub standard. Selling, delivery, warranty and after sale service became defining factors. Distributors were suddenly considered essential partners in helping the manufacturer win and maintain customer loyalty.

Phase #4 (Current) Quality products are worth the money. The keyword is Value.

Quality has evolved to the point where it is determined exclusively by the consumer's perception of value. $V=Q/P$ (Value equals quality divided by price). Consumers are delighted only when they receive benefits beyond what they expect for the amount paid. Today's economic winners track the customers' evolving perception of value.

"Some things are worth fighting for, particularly the success of your primary relationship. Knowing how to fight fair is essential." Art

The words intimacy and intimidate share the Latin root "intima," meaning between. The potential for love/hate between people increases as they get closer to each other and marriage is as close as it gets. Couples typically begin with the aspiration of sharing love, trust and respect. But living together can also create tension, frustration and disillusionment.

FIGHTING FAIR

The quality of life that exists between the adult partners of a primary relationship depends on skill as well as affection. Healthy couples are not afraid to voice their anger, fear or pain, with a passion equal to their expression of love for each other. They accept conflict as a natural shadow in a loving relationship. When people suppress passion during a negative exchange, they unwittingly retard their ability to express their love passionately. Turning negative passion off like a light switch contributes to relationship disease. The following suggestions will help you develop the mindset, environment and the skill of fighting fair.

Develop a fair fight strategy in advance:

First agree on how, when and where to fight. Make a list and discuss each other's dirty tricks:

Yelling or becoming volatile. Crying and other wounded duck routines. Dispensing the evil eye or cold shoulder. Not listening. Making light of the situation. Resurfacing old issues. Walking away. Withholding sex. Describing character flaws. Transferring responsibility or blame to others. Justifying your position. Acquiescing. Agree not to use any of the unfair behaviors listed above.

Create a time out signal that indicates when you suspect that a dirty trick is being used.

A 10 step fight fair process:
- Agree that a fight is taking place.
- Select a suitable place and time to fight.
- Review the dirty tricks list and time out signal.
- Fight fair, don't use or accept dirty tricks.
- After the initial ventilating is complete, repeat what you think the other person is asking for.
- Clarify as required.
- Own as much responsibility as you possibly can for causing and resolving the conflict.
- Seek for a win/win position where both you and your partner benefit.
- When its done, make a formal declaration that the fight is over.
- Let go of any remaining negative feelings and get on with life.

"Adults will often refuse to accept new information and cling to outdated think-
ing or dysfunctional ways of doing things." Art

Knowing has become a liability because in a rapidly changing world it is impossible for any single human being to stay on top of everything. Those of us who are long in the tooth will find it difficult to accept, but not knowing has become the new foundation of power.

ADULT EDUCATION

But don't run off because you haven't got a clue and declare your-self a genius. To succeed you must replace your not knowing mind-set with a not knowing attitude, plus a process for finding out and taking action faster than the competition.

Children start life with a blank page and no pretense. They have a vacuum between their ears that human nature struggles to keep full. This space is the reason children are capable of rapidly assimilating information and new skills. Adults are less responsive because their creative space is already full. Adults must unlearn before they can learn.

Unlearning for most of us does not happen as frequently as our rap-idly changing world demands. As parents, managers, professionals and trades or service people, we are heavily invested in preserving the status quo of what we know. Adults resist change because learn-ing screws up knowing and they erroneously assume that knowing remains a source of power.

Just because you graduated with a good education, mastered a chal-lenging career, married successfully, have close friends and are securely invested, doesn't mean you will coast through the rest of your life unscathed. To succeed you must learn to let go. In other words, you must unlearn.

Learning is analogous to the nose cone on a space rocket. A powerful force is needed to push new ways of doing things into a self-sustaining orbit beyond the gravitational pull of the status quo. Multiple launches will be required during your lifetime. To reinvent one's self, old stuff must first be removed.

In the space industry, recovering obsolete or damaged nose cones has become a necessity. There is space junk in your life as well. Obsolete careers, relationships, products or ideas present an increasing hazard. To accommodate what will be a never-ending stream of change, successful people will develop and maintain their personal equivalent of NASA's reusable Challenger launch vehicle. The primary benefit of adult education is learning to get rid of space junk and implementing the process of continuous learning.

" Organizations and employees who weathered North America's restructuring storm are no longer prepared to accept paternalistic or dependent relationships. A new more mature form of trust, built on mutual respect and sound principles is needed to make the people side of business work in a restructured workplace. "
Art

Decision making is becoming increasingly difficult. There are more choices and staggering amounts of conflicting information out there. Strangers seem to be taking more and more control over our lives. These days when somebody says "trust me," my knee jerk response is usually the opposite. The good news is that I get into fewer scrapes. The bad news, is that I have become cynical and resistant to change.

MATURE TRUST

Our capitalist society is thriving in a Global economy that provides jobs and access to a plethora of affordable products. Most of what I buy is provided by people over whom I have no influence. I open packages of processed food, trusting that the contents will not harm me. I travel busy highways filled with cars that may or may not be road worthy. Each car piloted by a nameless driver has an unknown capacity to operate within the rules. To get along in this complex world, I have no choice but to trust in spite of the risk. How is one to know when trust is well founded? By the same token, why should people that I don't know trust me?

Children have no choice but to place their survival in the hands of parents and caregivers. But youngsters begin to discern and learn to fend for themselves as maturity makes more options available. Today's adult is offered variety beyond the wildest imagination of previous generations. In spite of the options, too many adults blindly accept whatever comes along with a childlike naiveté.

Striking a balance between healthy skepticism and blind faith is the best we can do to protect ourselves and experience life in a meaningful way. You can improve the odds inherent with trusting others.

Strive to earn the trust of at least one human being each day. Hopefully, what goes around will come around. As the old song says, "if everyone lit just one little candle, what a bright world this would be."

The following check list will help you foster mature trust:

T......tell the whole truth without making others feel small.

R..... respect the internal greatness of others and never underestimate their potential.

U..... understand what others are trying to say even when they are not communicating well.

S...... seek for an honorable intention behind the actions of others, particularly when they fail.

T......take the initiative to confront when necessary, but don't play win/lose with others.

"Depression is a signal that all is not well. If sufferers take action and get medical attention, the experience can be a positive watershed." Art

Holidays such as Christmas and Thanksgiving are supposed to be happy occasions. But for many they bring back painful reminders of unfulfilled childhood expectations.

DEPRESSION

People can be negatively influenced by the weather. For example sudden mid winter thaws brought on by warm Chinook winds, the changing seasons or a prolonged absence of sunlight. Other mood altering triggers include physical or emotional traumas and reaction to the anniversaries of life altering events such as the death of a loved one. At least one half of all North Americans will experience depression at some point in their lives. The majority of those affected will not recognize it. Some develop chronic depression that feels more like a dull ache than psychological pain. Chronic conditions ebb at times but without help, depression seldom goes away. Many have been depressed for so long, they have no idea what it feels like to be normal. Situations often leave people unhappy. But there is a marked difference between the absence of happiness and depression. Sufferers lose focus and are unable to resolve even simple problems.

People fear being labeled as depressed. This societal mindset is unfortunate because when treated, depression seldom leaves a permanent scar like more socially acceptable stress related conditions such as ulcers or heart trouble. Although depression induces slowness in action and thought, the condition is far from passive. Fear and pain (often beyond the afflicted party's awareness) is always hiding in the shadows. A particular tone of voice, or specific words, behaviors and objects, can unleash without warning, powerful unresolved feelings. Depression typically causes the sufferer to withdrawal from social interaction. But isolation is an effect not the cause.

It is unfair and dangerous to expect depressed people to recover on their own. The disease causes a loss of perspective. Because the brain has been chemically altered, medical attention is an essential first step in the healing process. Never hesitate to intervene and do what it takes to get an ailing friend or loved one to a doctor. It could be a matter of life and death.

Common symptoms:

Changes in sleep or eating patterns, the lowering of sexual drive or function, losing interest in previously enjoyable activities, crying or ongoing sadness, feelings of intense boredom or helplessness, insecurity or a sense of worthlessness, self-medicating with drugs or alcohol.

Treatment:

New anti depressant drugs without the debilitating or addictive side effects of earlier varieties are available. The benefit of medical treatment is that patients quickly experience a sense of wellness. They usually regain sufficient clarity to make life adjustments that eventually produce wellness.

"Adults do dumb things at times. But the experience can resurrect childlike joy and happiness as well." Art

LOST SOLES

Following the lead of my buddies and purchasing a 4 seater jet boat proved that the only difference between men and boys is the size, price and speed of their toys. My wife took the wind out of my sails by naming the vessel and adorning its hull with oversized identification decals. Looking cool while piloting a boat called Arthur's Mid-life Crisis is next to impossible.

Manufacturers suggest that jet boats are popular because of safety (they have no prop) and a 3" draw to accommodate shallow running. Not true. People (like me) buy jet boats because they are fast, loud and smell like the Indiana 500 on race day. Their primary selling feature, however, is that you can almost stand them on their ear in the water.

After a few days practice, my buddies and I discovered how to spin out like a frizbee, by turning a tight circle at 50 miles an hour. Another neat trick was to hit the reverse at top speed-submerging unsuspecting passengers who didn't know the boat had an automatic bailer and was unsinkable.

After a few months, a couple of crashes and some broken ribs, the novelty wore off. Tales of daring exploits were becoming few and far between.

An off-handed question, "think they'd make it across Georgian Bay?" (100 miles of open water) was somehow transformed into a commitment. We waited for a calm sea, then 2 jet boats and 4 half wits, loaded with food, libations, radios, satellite navigation devices and extra gas cans; set sail for distant shores. We filed our route with the coast guard but not our wives (they would never have let us go had they known).

Georgian Bay is reputed to be the second bluest body of water in the world. Had assessors been with us that day, it would have overtaken the Danube and become #1. The challenge was daunting, the scenery magnificent, conversations titillating and the trip almost trouble free. About mid point we stopped to refuel. A roll on the water made hitting the funnel difficult and in the process, I spilled gas on the floor. No problem I thought, nobody was smoking the ignition was off and I'd wipe it up after I finished.

The boat's owner (I was wise enough to leave mine at home) suddenly screamed, "what's that?" I turned, expecting to see Mobey Dick. What had caught his attention was shoes disintegrating beneath my feet. Synthetic soles in contact with spilled gas, transformed into a sticky black goo covering the bottom of the boat. It took hours to clean up the mess. We eventually made it to the other side and spent a raucous night embellishing the details of our quest. The next day we wisely trailered the boats home.

This experience attached new meaning to the notion, "lost souls at sea." I vowed before God and The Mrs. Herself that I would never again gamble my fate in a small boat on open waters. But never is a long time and at 55, I don't remember so good.

"Its tough to play the game when everybody else is playing by different rules."
Art

Remaining competitive in a global economy has necessitated major changes in the way businesses organize people for work. Few communities have escaped the impact of downsizing, mergers, relocation or acquisition. Everybody knows of a friend, relative or neighbor who has lost a job during these turbulent times.

UNDERSTANDING THE ABC'S OF A RESTRUCTURED WORKPLACE

Although the workplace has been restructured, many people are still operating from an industrial age mindset that is no longer based in reality. When one looks at a changing world through an outdated assumption, everything looks insane. Alice experienced similar perceptual distortions during her visit to Wonderland. Potential winning strategies pass undetected when people cling to outdated attitudes, beliefs and ways of doing things. Sufferers are often despondent because "in tune" friends, family and neighbors can't live up to their misguided expectations. The following ABC's of employment are based on a new way of looking at the world that represents the workplace as it really is.

A -attitude:

You must reinvent yourself and your relationships on an ongoing basis to meet the demands of an evolving workplace. Think of yourself as owning your own corporation and working under contract to a paying customer. As long as your employer (customer) has work and pays adequately for your service, the partnership is viable. Customer relationships are not entitlements. They can end without warning. So routinely assess your customer's (employer), short and long term need for the work you do. You must also evaluate your customer's ongoing capacity and willingness to pay.

Your personal corporation has only two strategies to choose from:
(a) Provide multiple products/services to a single market by arranging a long term contract with a single organization. The contract should evolve as required to keep yourself right priced.
(b) Seek multiple markets for your product/service by arranging short-term contracts with several employers. You go where you can get the best deal, moving as opportunities present themselves.

B-boundaries:

Paternal loyalty to and from organizations must be replaced by a reality-based partnership that exists only when all parties are profiting from the relationship. Employers and employees may still develop an intimate alliance but everybody accepts it as a business relationship-not part of an extended family. Accept personal responsibility for the security and profitability of your own career and retirement plan. Never assume there will be permanent employment from any organization. It is self-defeating to hitch your wagon to a star that could burn out or change positions on you.

C-collaboration:

Permanent teams are making way for ad hoc groups that form and disband as required. Transient teaming is a watchword in the new economy. It demands new skills. You must learn how to:
• start, maintain and end a project.
• embrace new concepts, people and ways of doing things.
• choose how and when to confront.
• take the initiative to resolve conflicts.
• trust others and earn their trust.
• ask for help.
• earn your keep in a demanding environment

"Winston Churchill spent more time deciding what not to say than he did writing the first drafts of a speech. He is renown for saying more with less, but he had to work at it." Art

KISS (keep it simple stupid) is a directive I find myself chanting after things are out of control. Would that I had the wisdom to incorporate simplicity at the beginning of a task or interpersonal exchange.

THE VALUE OF SIMPLICITY

Simplification rule # 1 Let go of unused possessions:
Unused possessions use up valuable time and energy. George Carlin made light of our attachment to things by reducing the meaning of life to a process of collecting "stuff". He suggested that babies become toddlers when they grow tired of stuffing their diapers and discover a better way. After trouser pockets fill with rocks, snails and other captivating objects, children move their storage center to the bedroom. Once the bedroom fills with treasure (during late adolescence), its time to move up the evolutionary ladder and acquire private digs. The young adult then starts accumulating really expensive stuff. Young people eventually propagate and humanity's stuff collecting torch is passed to another generation.
Knowing how and when to let go of things is essential to healthy human development. Beginnings are not possible without endings. Clinging to outgrown possessions, friendships, beliefs, attitudes and ideas make you root bound, like a plant trying to grow in a small pot. As an alternative to making New Years resolutions you never keep, justify the retention of articles and relationships that did not produce during the past year. You won't grow until you throw.
Simplification rule #2 Tell the whole truth with compassion:
Have you ever agreed to participate in an activity when you had no desire to do so? Unwanted commitments are often made in lieu of

hurting the feelings of others. Learning to say no assertively but with respect, saves time and energy. Rehearse a response that will allow you to maintain control. The following works for me. "Thank you, it was considerate of you to think of including me but I'd rather not." Offering an explanation for your decision is an option but not essential. Resist implying there could be a next time if you don't mean it.

Simplification rule # 3 Listen more than you speak:

People who listen seldom get in over their heads. If you avoid getting caught up in the excitement of the moment, many complications will pass you by. Before responding, take the time to imagine possible outcomes and weigh positive possibilities against the potential risk. A useful assessment tool is Kurt Lewin's Force Field Analysis. Draw a line down the center of a page. List positive aspects of accommodating the request on one side and negative possibilities on the other side. Pay particular attention to the negatives. If the majority of them are manageable, your decision to commit should produce a successful experience.

"Five people looking at the same accident can see things differently. We look at the world through a lens that psychologists call a perceptual screen. Personal history plays a large part in what we notice." Art

Humans are incapable of viewing reality. What we see is filtered through a prejudiced perspective.

REALITY IS JUST ONE PERSON'S OPINION

We make sense of the outside world by interpreting information through a perceptual screen. Our highly personalized way of looking at things is based on assumptions accepted as unconditional truth during childhood. A perceptual screen helps us make better decisions by using past experience to discern opportunity from danger. But a perceptual screen can also be a liability. It restricts us to seeing things one way-our own way. If the history of an adult includes childhood trauma, his or her reality could be skewed towards seeing potential threats everywhere. A negatively conditioned perspective generates anti social behavior, anxiety, depression and low self-esteem.

Perspective is formed because of the meaning we attach to people, places, things, beliefs and ideas. For example, when humans fall in love their sense of reality is dramatically changed. The perspective of lovers is chemically altered by racing hormones. They see a world in which the object of their affection can do no wrong. But after the honeymoon, warts in the relationship inevitably appear. Another example of perceptual screening is stereotyping people we are close to. Developing a fixed assumption about how others are feeling, why they behave as they do and most destructively, what they are and are not capable of, overlooks the potential of people to change. Unwittingly, we often keep loved ones in their place.

As humans mature, some crystallize their thinking around a fixed perceptual screen, limiting themselves to an unchanging interpretation of reality. Others choose a path of perpetual growth, continuing to try new things until the day they die. They remain open to fresh ideas and listen to the opinion of others. The choice is yours; continued learning from 75 years of varied experience or one year of learning experience repeated 75 times.

"It is difficult to live up to adult expectations that are childhood fantasies. But at holiday time, many grown ups try to accomplish the impossible." Art

HOME FOR THE HOLIDAYS

The much touted theme "home for the holidays," produces powerful feelings of nostalgia blended with childlike anticipation. The festive season is supposed to be happy but a surprisingly large number of people experience annual bouts of sadness. Severe depression is quite common, causing more suicides than at any other time of the year.

Mental health experts suggest that holiday melancholia is caused primarily by unfulfilled expectations. In a mobile society, many people are alone. In the old days, it was standard practice to celebrate Christmas in a large multi-generation home. People suffer when their idealized (often fanciful) childhood memories clash with reality.

"Home for the holidays," is a comforting thought provided one has resolved the oft-unanswered question; "where is home?" Choosing which home to go to gets difficult after marriage. The issue is further complicated by parenthood and recurs later in life when adult children negotiate with each other for the attention of aging parents. The home factor not only presents newly married couples with the dilemma of conflicting family loyalties, they have to choose between differing holiday traditions. Elders often feel hurt when their holiday customs are rejected.

The festive season is an excellent time to step back and let the next generation do its thing. Turning over traditional responsibilities at this time of the year can be a powerful right of passage for the entire family.

Tips for improving holiday wellness:

- The festive season is about honoring new life. Advance traditions that will benefit the young.
- Use the holidays to execute rights of passage. Wherever possible, transfer custom and responsibility to the next generation.
- Support other children if you don't have access to youngsters of your own.
- Disadvantaged adults could also use a touch of kindness during the holidays.
- If you feel lonely, don't be afraid to seek out the company of others. For example, attend a neighborhood church and take in their pageants.
- Plan in advance to involve family or friends.
- Use personal experience (good or bad) from festive seasons past, to create a positive holiday atmosphere for yourself and others.
- Don't be afraid to give or ask for help.
- Put yourself out there and it will make a difference.

Research has identified touch as the most powerful and rewarding form of human contact. From the moment of birth, healthy individuals enjoy activity that puts them in touch with other people.

PUTTING
"THE TOUCH"
ON PEOPLE

Visitors to a public library were interviewed as part of a study on the effects of human contact. The only variable was that some participants were touched physically by the librarian. A seemingly accidental brushing of hands took place during the exchange of books. Those who were touched, reported a level of satisfaction from that day's library experience much higher than visitors who had not been touched. Interestingly, most did not remember the librarian's contiguity.

Children need the gift of loving touch from other humans in order to develop both physically and mentally. Orphaned Romanian babies left unattended in their cribs, except for twice daily non-contact feeding and diaper changes, were unable to raise their heads or sit like healthy children of the same age. People will seek out human contact, one way or another. Ignored youngsters act out because reprimand and spankings are less painful than having no contact at all.

Well-adjusted children instinctively maximize human contact during play. They will typically hold hands, wrestle, and constantly touch each other during conversation, particularly when making an important point. Healthy kids are natural huggers who bless friends and loved ones regularly with warm embraces-until inhibition and uncertainty sets in. Early conditioning in the home is the primary determinant of an adult's willingness to accept and offer physical contact. People deprived of touching while living with their family of origin, find hugging difficult and uncomfortable. Unwittingly, we are making it even more difficult for the next generation. For example, our paranoia with sexual preditors is isolating children from experiencing healthy forms of human touch. Teaching children to fear strangers is unwarranted because the dangers purported are not supported by statistics. The majority of child molestations are perpetrated by family members and individuals known to the parents.

Everybody needs and most people welcome human contact. Success depends on selecting the most appropriate method of "putting the touch" on others. Appropriateness will be determined exclusively by the recipient. It is uncaring and dangerous to assume that your threshold of intimacy will be acceptable to others.

"Putting your trust in a higher power is a giant leap of faith. Many of us ignore the benefits of prayer and meditation until we face an emergency and events move beyond our control." Art

THE POWER OF PRAYER AND MEDITATION

An over supply of oil had destroyed real estate values in my area. Local businesses needed an undertaker more than they needed a consultant so I decided to relocate my practice. Moving the company was a breeze compared to the difficulties I experienced trying to sell the house. Ours was one of thousands being offered at fire sale prices and it had been listed for months.

My wife and I were sensitive to an emotional trauma facing our oldest daughter who would soon enter a new school and meet new kids; knowing she was going to be uprooted and forced to do it all over again. Reluctantly, we sent her back east to stay with my sister. But the family move didn't follow immediately as we had planned.

The Mrs. Herself and I were sitting on the patio. It was a melancholy Thanksgiving weekend. Our daughter was away from home, the house wasn't selling and we were stretched to the breaking point financially. A beautiful fall day was little consolation to our grief. I called our real estate agent who said there was little chance of anything happening over a long weekend.

"We need help," I said to my wife as I limped away hang-doggedly to lick my wounds. The prayer I offered was nothing special, just a plea to protect and comfort my distressed family. I sat alone for some time when suddenly a feeling of exhilaration came over me.

I had a daydream that was so vividly clear, I had to share the experience. I rejoined my wife on the patio and exclaimed mockingly, "It's all looked after. We'll sell the house today and get our price. The buyer is a guy with dark hair. He'll fall in love with the fireplace and have some concerns about the back yard." After blurting it out, I pulled a ball cap over my eyes and fell asleep.

Within the hour, an agent called wanting to show the house. I turned to my wife jokingly, "there's #1." The agent arrived with a dark haired man in tow. "That's #2," I smiled. A few minutes later, the agent stuck her head out of the door and asked, "does the hardware stay with the fireplace?" My wife and I were speechless. Finally, the agent and his client said goodbye. "All they missed was the back yard," I mused just as the dark haired man stuck his head over our gate. "Are there electrical outlets in the back yard?" he asked.

That afternoon we signed a deal close to the asking price and soon after my family was reunited. My wife and I believe we were blessed with a miracle that day.

"Primitive peoples typically resist having their picture taken because they fear their spirit will become trapped in the likeness. When we assign a name to something, we no longer have to deal with its essence. Children know instinctively that conceptual facsimiles are no substitute for the real thing." Art

THE WONDER OF IT ALL

The success of Thomas Moore's book, Care of the soul and James Redfield's best selling Celestine series, demonstrates North America's renewed interest in exploring the spiritual side of life. Prior to accepting technology's mechanistic perspective, people addressed God and nature with awe and reverence. Full of themselves, scientists at the turn of the century believed that everything could and should be explained. Their attitude caused us to lose a bit of what it means to be human.

Our ability to appreciate being alive physically and spiritually often decreases as intellectual understanding increases. For example, sunsets can lose their majesty under the cold hard light of a scientific explanation about the characteristics of light refraction. The magic of falling in love fades in relevance when considered only from the perspective of racing hormones and pleasure producing endorphins. And the joy of Christmas is diminished once we stop believing in Santa Clause.

Much has been accomplished because of scientific discipline; but something has been lost along the way. Spirituality and wonder has for too long taken a back seat to science. But there is good news looming. Albert Einstein started a renaissance when he blew apart

Isaac Newton's mechanistic laws of the universe, setting the stage for others to introduce the new science of quantum physics. Einstein's hypothesis that light traveled without medium by distorting space changed our long held understanding of gravity. Even the precision of time was discounted when Einstein's Theory of Relativity was validated scientifically, using clocks and jet aircraft. Scientists now suggest that humans flying into space at high speeds, age slower during their flight than the rest of us.

The gap between science and spirituality is closing. Good science no longer requires spiritual atrophy. Today, there are fewer experienced scientists who are mechanistic in their beliefs. Most have acknowledged happenings that defy professional understanding several times during their career. In other words they have witnessed miracles.

Personal development based solely on mechanistic perspective, misses the boat. Athletes and artists refer to being "in the zone," where time seems to slow and the mind/body performs beyond assumed physical limits. Superior performers credit their skill to heredity, practice and hard work, but many also believe that their peak performances are spiritual in nature.

Beautiful scenery, great works of art or inspired writings, have no purpose or meaning until the individual experiences the grace of melding so completely with the subject that an "ah ha," or spiritual awakening takes place.

Since the beginning of time people have debated the foundation of faith. In Judao Christian traditions, arguments abound between fundamentalist and liberal attitudes. Depending on one's perspective, the Bible is either the direct word of God or a collection of writings containing profound wisdom that has withstood the test of time. Among those who call themselves believers are many who take the Word literally and others who with equal passion, use the Bible metaphorically. Regardless of orientation, both groups use the scriptures to moderate their lives and worship God. The common denominator is a shared belief in a higher purpose and pursuing the integration of mind, body and spirit.

"Establishing personal boundaries that strike a balance between protection and the accommodation of personal growth is an essential element in human wellness. People who barricade themselves from life, suffer as much as those who leave themselves vulnerable." Art

Wall:
(n) barrier, bastion, battlement, bulwark (v) to enclose
Boundary:
(n) border, frontier, line of demarcation

FROM WALLS TO BOUNDARIES

The price of admission to life includes the necessity of making either or decisions such as to join or detach, accept or eject or to fight or flee. Some try in vain to avoid the responsibility of decision making by building walls to separate their comfortable "what is" from a scary "what could be." You are in the presence of personal walls every time you hear the words never or always. Business people call this self-defeating strategy a fortress mentality. Sufferers cling to the status quo at all costs, hoping they can wait it out and that their problems will go away. The construction of walls usually marks the beginning of the end for people and organizations. The Berlin wall is a classic example. The communists couldn't keep people in or democracy out.

We must however, defend ourselves against potential aggressors. Naïve trust and vulnerability are as great a threat as building a fortress. The key to success, is knowing how to develop and maintain boundaries. Boundaries signal expectations and define your limits to the outside world. They also stimulate a call to action when violated. Boundaries are more effective than walls because they are permeable. They protect yet allow you to stay in touch with what's going on outside. As well, boundaries are less threatening to the outside world. When outsiders are not allowed to know what is going on behind a wall, they can become paranoid and hostile.

The term boundary conjures up an image of frontier. This positive paradigm stimulates creativity and controlled growth. Boundaries can be tested and altered to meet changing conditions. For example, people who fear travelling might participate in day trips with trusted friends. Low risk experiments will either reinforce the validity of their boundary or provide an incentive to expand horizons. It is essential for the young to test boundaries in order to develop and grow. They seldom work at maintaining the status quo because they have little to lose and everything to gain.

"We can't prevent father time from extracting his toll on aging bodies. All we can do is exercise, stretch, rest and adhere to the principles of sound nutrition. But humans have more influence over their mental agility than they typically use."
Art

The human spirit is packaged in a remarkably flexible form when it first arrives. At birth, the skull consists of separate bone plates that eventually knit together to form the brain's protective shield. Our species would be in mortal danger if babies had to travel the birth canal with a rigid skull. All the other joints do not form completely until the human body stops growing.

WHEN FORM KILLS FUNCTION

After a brief interlude of physical perfection that ends during the mid 20s, father time starts to extract his toll on the human body. The price of a long life is the loss of stamina and flexibility. Our calcified form eventually limits function. Unfortunately, many people also believe that mental rigidity is a non-negotiable companion to the aging process.

Brain diseases such as Alzheimer's cause degeneration of mental capacity. But aging is not a disease. Nature makes a valiant attempt to care for mental wellness during an entire life span. Humans use only a small percentage of their available brain-power. If seniors are healthy and engaged intellectually, mental capacity can be maintained. Seniors also have an invaluable asset called experience that is denied young adults. Experience combined with wisdom is essential to a culture's long term survival. In most societies (our own not included), elders are held in high esteem because of their significant role in nurturing and mentoring the young.

Adults are typically preoccupied with here and now issues such as accommodation, safety, food and procreation. Historically, successful cultures rely on elders to provide spiritual direction, interpretation and the administration of law, health care and child development. Studies have demonstrated that senility can be retarded and in some cases even reversed when seniors have daily contact with children. Here and now adult concerns are of little consequence to children and they are of less interest to seniors. The first and third generation have much in common. Communication possibilities are enhanced because they share a less materialistic mindset.

Carl Jung deviated from his colleague Sigmund Freud, by including spirituality in his study of the human condition. One of Jung's conclusions was that well-adjusted humans spend the first half of their life competing in the material world. After achieving a measure of success, they experience a transformation that focuses on spiritual development. Jung implied that balance requires a complete lifetime. People who seek spiritual growth before they are materially fulfilled and people who chase material gain beyond mid life, often feel empty and cheated at the end of the day. Nature's design calls for increased spiritual growth as the body winds down.

"Fairy tales have been used by humanity since the dawn of time. They appeal to the youngster in all of us. In my consulting practice, if an issue was contentious, I often used stories to make a point. Story telling is useful because it short circuits critical adult minds." Art

Our society is attempting to legislate social harmony rather than asking people to honor commandments that have withstood the test of time. Civil harmony is best accomplished when people adhere to guidelines such as the golden rule. America's founding fathers included many God centered statements in the constitution because they understood the necessity of intrinsic values.

DEATH OF A VILLAGE

Once upon a time a group of industrious people lived in a beautiful village they had built with their own hands. Traveling from far off lands, these pioneering villagers had invested an entire lifetime trying to create a better life for their children. There were places of equal beauty in the old world, but the villagers made their home different by adopting rules that protected personal freedoms and equal opportunity. Their declaration of rights reflected a deep faith in God, an innate distrust of institutionalized power and a belief that real freedom demanded personal involvement.

It was understood that neighbors would help neighbors and that everybody would contribute time and resources to maintain essential services. These people built a marvelous village and collectively managed community affairs. They chose leaders carefully. Successive generations prospered and the village became the envy of the world. The inhabitants became wealthy and they hired newcomers to work the fields and factories. Immigrants poured into the village seeking a better way of life. There was enough for all and everybody assumed that prosperity would go on forever.

But people started forgetting that success came from strict adherence to the village rules. They denied that God centered values formed the heart of their charter of rights and that the Word provided an essential source of timeless wisdom. Both owners and workers were too busy to participate in matters of faith and stopped honoring their long-standing personal commitment to the community. People no longer lived by the golden rule; "do unto others as you would have them do unto you." Unethical strangers stepped in to take advantage of the chaos.

The opportunists discovered that profits could be extracted by pitting neighbor against neighbor. They focused on details, not the spirit of law and misrepresented facts to advance their cause. Freedom-limiting amendments were added to the law. Legislation stimulated profit, so the opportunists worked hard to get their own elected. The opportunists soon formed a majority in government and they quietly assumed control of public life. Business owners and workers were so preoccupied with making a living, they didn't notice that a privileged club had assumed power.

More money was needed to pay for a growing bureaucracy so taxes were raised each year. Special entitlements were granted to vocal minorities led by the opportunists. The villagers grew more and more dependent on receiving handouts from the government. They didn't comprehend that the gifts were coming out their own pockets-paid for by taxes. Without control over their own money, the people gradually relinquished power. Soon the opportunists viewed themselves as the village masters, not servants of the people.

Villagers no longer felt a sense of ownership towards their homeland. Violence and crime was running rampant. Although many complained about society being out of control, few were willing to challenge the opportunists and run for public office. People quit talking to each other and stopped compromising. Instead, they litigated. Villagers lost respect for the rights of others. It soon became every man for himself.

A group of concerned villagers tried to teach school children the spiritual values that their village was founded on. But fearing a loss of power, the opportunists created new laws to prevent them from doing so. Because the villagers were not allowed to discuss the faith of their founding fathers in public, fewer and fewer people lived by the rules. No longer influenced by values, village leaders tried to restore order by being tough on crime. But in the process, they unwittingly eliminated the rights and freedoms of innocent people. The once prosperous village was dying and nobody lived happily ever after.

"The media has crossed the line from providing insight and useful information to offering mindless drivel." Art

A once honorable profession, succumbing to financial pressure, is now focusing on ratings rather than the pursuit of truth. The media has crossed the line from journalism to entertainment. Unlike their disciplined predecessors, today's investigative reporters would rather shock than inform.

BETWEEN FACT AND FICTION

Repetitive exposure to behaviors falling outside of what society considers acceptable desensitizes people and influences their understanding of right and wrong. The media is unwittingly moving us towards the toleration of violence, sexual permissiveness and the normalization of alternate life styles - at the expense of traditional family values. The media however, accepts no responsibility for the lowering of community standards. Media moguls are the moral equivalent of drug dealers and their undiscerning audiences have become entertainment junkies, unwilling to think any further than the next fix.

The news has become entertainment. America experienced nationwide withdrawal symptoms when the O.J. Simpson trial ended. Audiences felt abandoned without a daily barrage of analysts filling prime time news. Our kids are being conditioned to seek forms of entertainment that are at and beyond the parameters of civility. The Gulf war was a media event. To the desensitized, just an exciting video game on prime time, complete with commercials and color commentary. Audiences woke up the next day and like junkies; went on about their business in blissful denial that real people had been killed.

The following solicits your personal involvement in the restoration of a values based society:

• Reassess your adult responsibility to future generations. Set an example and encourage others to experience life as discerning participants rather than passive spectators.

- Fight both the supply and consumption side of your family's entertainment addiction. Exert parental control over what your children watch and read.
- Teach your children critical thinking skills and through personal example, promote a healthy skepticism of sensationalized media coverage.
- Boycott productions that, in the name of entertainment, promote unacceptable behavior and stretch attitudes beyond the borders of civility.
- Warn your children that people become what they consume.

"An experiment that demonstrates the properties of magnetism helps to clarify what happens to a human being when mind, body and spirit are integrated. Like iron filings influenced by a magnet, many of life's trials and tribulations will sort themselves out if we stay centered." Art

When your car is out of alignment, inevitably things will start going wrong. Tires wear unevenly, front struts weaken, break pads deteriorate and shimmies at high speed loosen car joints, screws and your peace of mind. Unaligned vehicles tend to squeal during tight turns and steering wheels go off center (along with your disposition). Alignment problems within the human body affect people in a similar way. When your back is out it can cause nerve damage, wear and tear on connective tissue, organ deterioration and muscle atrophy; not to mention excruciating pain.

ALIGNMENT

Cars can't align themselves. Correction requires an intervention from an external force, such as a mechanic using a diagnostic computer. The same holds true when it comes to aligning the human system. The body can't be aligned by its occupant in every case. No amount of exercise will correct a structural fault because muscle groups adjust and work around the disorder. Exercise can reinforce rather than alleviate an alignment problem. Chiropractors physically manipulate the spine. Medical research has proven their process (called an alignment) to be more effective than drugs, rest and most surgeries. Physiotherapists also intervene by forcing damaged and weakened muscles to move beyond limitations imposed by a sickness or injury. When muscles are restricted in range of movement for an extended period of time, the human system adapts by realigning other parts of the anatomy to accommodate the injury.

Continued reinforcement of the original disorder can create a permanent disability.

Healthy people work at keeping mind, body and spirit aligned throughout their entire lifetime. This ongoing process requires both internal and external interventions. God, family, friends, professionals, books, workshops, and lessons learned from experience combine with vision, commitment and tenacity to assist in the alignment of a healthy human being.

How to align:

- For the mind (nutrition)

  Fasting improves your capacity to control what you ingest in the way of food and liquids. It also disciplines you to regulate your acceptance of ideas, attitudes and beliefs.

- For the body (stamina & power)

  Exercise prepares the body for movement and increases its capacity to carry a heavy load. A well-conditioned body knows how to relieve stress. Stress reduction prevents the mind from overreacting to the fight /flight survival instincts that produce stress related disease.

- For the spirit (will to win desire to belong)

  Prayer and meditation helps maintain focus. It provides a sense of direction and can fuel one's desire to participate in life. Turning to a higher power as a source of strength and wisdom helps people hold themselves together.

"Aligning the mind, body and spirit enhances one's ability to contribute and fully experience the joys of daily living. But each of us must pass through several phases of aging that require major adjustments." Art

THE CYCLE OF LIFE

I facilitated business planning workshops in a past life. As a management consultant I asked executives to assess the maturity of their industry. This step helped them assess the viability of strategic options. To explain the concept of maturity cycles I compared business to the evolution of a human being. The Biblical passage, "for everything there is a season," hits the nail on the head, People from all four phases of life's cycle should attend to their unique responsibilities, while honoring the contribution of other groups.

Phase #1 Embryonic

Most of what we need to know to survive as a human being is learned before the age of five. Until puberty it is appropriate for children to spend their time engaged in play, nature's most effective learning process. Because play is typically spontaneous, it promotes the development of creativity and imagination. Many parents ruin child play by emphasizing organization (as they have done in sports and the performing arts). Because we do too much for children, many of life's essential learnings are missed. For example, how to start and end things, how to choose sides, make up and enforce rules, use ingenuity in place of missing equipment and most importantly, how to shift to something else once the fun or learning stops. During the embryonic phase, anything goes as long as it isn't life threatening. Mistakes are expected. If 3 year-old Mary decides to moon Aunt Margret, nobody (except for the embarrassed parents) gets overly upset. Most people would be amused because they understand that childhood is an appropriate time to experiment and test boundaries. New industries like the internet often fail because they are measured against mature businesses such as the telephone system. Childhood development is retarded when kids are forced to act like little adults.

Phase #2 Growth

At some point the humorous antics of growing children cease to amuse. The community starts asking penetrating questions such as, "when are you going to grow up and act your age?" Societal rules should be rigorously enforced before fledglings are kicked out of the nest and expected to fly on their own as a contributing citizen. Puberty to the mid 20s is a time for investing in one's future. At this stage of life, the potential for big pay-offs from the fruits of study, work and social experience are huge. So too are the pay-backs when a teenager screws up. The life of an adolescent should not be all fun and games.

Childlike behavior from an adolescent is inappropriate because the consequences of the latter's mistakes are far more serious. Rebellious activities such as drug and alcohol consumption, unsafe sex, vandalism and reckless driving, place severe burdens on the community. Infractions should be dealt with harshly as an essential part of the learning process. Understanding and civility must develop during this phase of life or it may never be acquired. Important lessons include:

- the law of consequence-you will get out of life what you put in.
- the necessity of self sufficiency-nobody owes you a living.
- the value of fairness-playing by the rules is profitable in the long run.
- the reality of mortality-nothing and nobody lasts forever.

We are making the mistake of treating adolescents as though they were still in the embryonic stage. This oversight has caused many adults to continue acting like children.

Phase # 3 Maturity (adults)

Age 25 through to the mid 50s are the productive years. During this time, people procreate, raise families, build homes, create businesses, establish careers and form reputations. The old saying, "make hay while the sun shines," applies because adults are at the peak of physical and mental stamina. Dreaming and scheming should have taken place during adolescent growth years and meditating on the meaning of life will come later. Adulthood is prime time for taking action.

Mystics refer to balance as the essence of life. But effectiveness comes from balancing over the aggregate of all four of life's phases. People who attempt to balance within a specific phase such as maturity, typically accomplish very little. Balanced adults often become regretful in later years because of the opportunities that have passed them by. Hard work and long hours go with adult territory. Society is placing inappropriate and unfair expectations on people living life's most productive phase. For example, the assumption that day care should be a personal rather than communal responsibility. This wrong thinking is a recent innovation.

These days, many elders believe that daycare is unnatural and harmful. They erroneously assume that children should spend more time with parents. That was not common practice prior to the industrial revolution. Historically, senior members of the extended family (including aunts uncles and cousins) shouldered a large part of the responsibility for child rearing; while adults worked the fields and at other essential chores-every waking hour, six days a week.

Phase # 4 Aging (seasoned citizens)

The decline of physical prowess that has been creeping slowly since the age of 25, picks up speed at this point. It is self -defeating for elders to compete against standards established for the mature phase of life. But that doesn't mean elders have nothing to offer. Experience and perspective are invaluable assets that unfortunately are currently underutilized in our overly materialistic world.

There is a reason why much of what elders have provided since the dawn of time is no longer in demand. Prior to the written word, elders played an important role in child rearing. They were responsible for passing on history, values, visions of preferred futures and an understanding of community rules and responsibility. The industrial revolution destroyed the extended family and hastened the institutionalization of social services. Other influences that reduce the capacity of elders to make a meaningful contribution to community wellness include travel, the redistribution of wealth and the creation of isolated retirement communities.

There is a reemerging role for elders in this new information age. But age apartheid (retirement isolation to senior's communities with limited exposure to other age groups) must end before it can be realized. Children need additional support because both parents are once again, working full time. Elders must reassume nature's long established role of helping to care for and educating the young. If learning remains the exclusive domain of adult parents and teachers, society will continue the current preoccupation with material gain. Values training, the building of self-esteem, instruction on how to avoid danger and capitalize on life's opportunities are lessons best delivered by experienced people. Elders are essential to successful child rearing because they aren't overly distracted by adult pursuits.

"A good sense of humor is a valuable asset at any age. If you can't laugh you can't really live. Much of life is too absurd to be taken seriously." Art

Living under our bridges are trolls, cursed to living out their miserable lives as the gate-keepers of political correctness. Unfortunately, their stoic demeanor is just as contagious as laughter. Many are infected with a Troll like grumpy disposition. That's sad because humor is a welcomed shock absorber on this bumpy road called life.

TOO UP TIGHT TO TITTER

Three elderly gentlemen were sunning themselves on a park bench. The conversation was opened by the youngest, "at 94, I'm blessed with a good mind and excellent health, except for one problem. I have trouble passing my water. The plumbing isn't what it used to be." The group's second eldest responded, "I'm in good shape too, if it wasn't for my regularity problem." The trio's senior member shook his head in sympathy. "Before 7 o'clock every morning, I wizz like a race horse and have a bowel movement the nurses can set their watches by." "It must be wonderful to still have everything working out so well," the youngest reflected. "Not really" lamented the old timer, "I don't wake up until 9."

I hope you found some humor in that story. Many will frown because they believe it is politically incorrect to laugh at the funny things specific groups of people do, particularly the elderly. Others will feel insulted because I alluded to bodily functions. When did it become improper to laugh at life with all its silly ins and outs? In my opinion, the politically correct among us are too up tight. I won't go so far as to call them tight asses but it's a close call. Oops, there goes another vulgarity.

Is it my imagination or are people not laughing as much or as hard as they used to? My girls won't attend a humorous movie with their dear old Dad because he is prone to break into uncontrollable spasms of laughter. To their horror, it often happens when the rest of the theater is deathly quiet. What has changed? I remember friends and family falling off their chairs, tears streaming down happy faces as the masters such as Milton Berle, Red Skelton and Sid Caesar worked their magic. Every performance was live and visceral. Even the entertainers didn't know what to expect. Red Skelton took great delight in using hilarious ad-libs to break up unsuspecting guests. Everybody reveled in the spontaneity, screw-ups and all.

By contrast, today's comedy producers enhance audience response by superimposing canned laughter after the show is over. There is something wrong when audiences need technical support or a laughter cue. I don't want anybody meddling with my mirth.

People who can't laugh at life are incapable of laughing at themselves. Deprived of humanity's most effective release valve, pressure builds to the point where people become cynical and mean spirited. So come on folks, lighten up, bless yourselves with a few good old fashioned, belly shaking, nose snorting guffaws. Life's too short to spend it living under a bridge.

"The family provides an essential foundation for child rearing. Our society has become self absorbed to the point that many adults care more about their own gratification than the wellness of their innocent offspring." Art

Small boats by law are manufactured with sufficient buoyancy to stay afloat when capsized. Water safety specialists stress the importance of staying with a submerged vessel. Unnecessary deaths occur when accident victims try swimming for shores that appear closer than they really are. Hypothermia, waves and powerful currents can overtake even the most accomplished swimmer. For the security of our children, society would do well to promote a "stay with the family" message.

STAYING WITH A CAPSIZED FAMILY

Many discouraged spouses abandon their troubled relationship prematurely. Typically, both parties are ill prepared for the difficulties that lie ahead. Separation creates as many problems as it resolves. More-so if you consider the children. The real losers in a broken home are the children. I choose not to use politically correct terms such as the single parent home or alternate family. The word 'broken' is more representative.

Regardless of parental effort, permanent scars are imposed on the innocents of every failed marriage. Even loving parents shatter the emotional wellness of children when they divorce. Kids pay a price for the broken commitment of their parents. Lessening the impact of marital separation on children requires maturity, clear thinking and a modicum of unselfish behavior-attributes demonstrably uncharacteristic of separating parents.

A recovery plan for separating parents:

• Entering a new relationship on the rebound dooms many second attempts because of unresolved issues that caused the first marriage to fail. Additional failures will damage the self esteem of children even further. Never leave a troubled relationship dumb. Dumb means not discovering and owning your fair share of responsibility. Left unattended, old problems resurface (once the honeymoon is over).

- Understand that judges and lawyers are not equipped or trained to counsel on the emotional wellness of their clients or involved children. Their job is to ensure personal security and litigate/negotiate custody and financial issues. They seldom advise clients to reconcile or chastise them for not honoring parental responsibility. A typical orientation is to get as much as they can for their client, regardless of the damage they may cause others. All too often, disgruntled and angry combatants seek revenge at the expense of their children.
- Work with a qualified marriage counselor to help you identify and own a fair share of responsibility for the separation. Marital breakdowns are seldom a one way street. Common personal failures include making poor choices, not growing in the relationship, demanding too much from a partner, differences in religious beliefs, financial problems, not leaving one's family of origin emotionally, sexual infidelity, lack of trust, not meeting obligations, immaturity and downright selfishness.
- Identify what you must change about yourself to help prevent a repeated relationship failure.
- Make every effort to reconcile with your estranged partner. A good marriage counselor will facilitate a conflict resolution process. Your ex will always be a part of your life. So establish clear boundaries and learn to get along for you own sake and more importantly, to support the emotional wellness of your children.

Agree to protect the children:
- Honor your children by living up to parental commitments and obligations.
- Atone for the pain you are causing and for the insecurity they will carry for the rest of their lives.
- Visit a professional counselor with your estranged spouse and agree on a joint parenting plan that clearly puts the children first. Formal training for separating spouses who have children is man-

dated by the courts in many communities. It's a great idea because the long-term impact of a shared parental initiative is encouraging to a child. Self-esteem is reinforced and children feel safer when they see separated parents working together on their behalf.

- Work with your ex-spouse to overcome the tendency of children to hold themselves responsible for marital problems. You can't remind children too often that the separation was not their fault. And that both parents still love them.
- Never do or say anything to diminish the estranged parent in the eyes of a child.
- Accept that you will never again be completely single. Make your new life fit the non-negotiable moral commitment to honor your parental responsibility. Make sure that potential new partners understand and will accept the extent of your commitment to your children.

"My wife often says, I can dress him up but I can't take him anywhere. Clothes do make the man, but in my case not as often as the Mrs. Herself would prefer."
Art

During a wilderness trip a couple of fishing buddies tired of their own cooking and decided to visit an exclusive resort. They made themselves as presentable as a limited wardrobe would allow and drove to town. The two were horrified to discover that a hotel dress code demanded the wearing of neck ties. Fortunately, one of the fishermen carried a spare tie in the glove box of his car. Annoyed at the restriction, the buddies approached the dinning room for another try. A black and orange striped tie on a plaid flannel shirt was reluctantly admissible but the second solution raised the maitre d's eyebrows. "We can't accept those battery cables around your neck as appropriate attire sir," he snapped condescendingly. "You'll accept anything I put around my neck or I'll sue you," barked the angry fisherman. "O.K" the disgruntled maitre d' retorted, "I'll make an exception this time, but don't you two try starting anything in there."

LIVING WITH DRESS CODES

On those rare occasions when the Mrs. Herself and I dress for a night on the town, I expect the establishments we frequent to preserve the environment we are paying for. But the process of enforcing dress codes can get out of hand. I was week ending at a quaint hotel in England. Rolling out of bed, jet lagged and irritable, I sleepwalked to the lobby for a much-needed Sunday morning coffee. There was only one dining facility. It was elaborate and empty. After waiting in vain, I ignored the "please wait to be seated" sign and sat down. A tux-garbed waiter appeared out of nowhere and with stiff upper lip advised me that I must dress for breakfast even though there were no other guests to offend. No room service was available at the hotel on weekends and breakfast alternatives in the immediate vicinity were non existent. Battery cables are never available when you really need them.

Researchers have proven that human behavior is influenced by attire. Students improve academic performance and get into less trouble when they are forced to wear a school uniform. Esprit de corps in the Canadian military suffered when the government tried to save money by standardizing army, navy and air force uniforms. The loss of tradition associated with dress codes had a powerful influence on troop morale. Establishments that enforce dress codes typically receive higher performance ratings from customers. They can also charge more because of their exclusive environment.

Advocates of restaurant dress codes would have us change the old saying; "you are what you eat," to "you are what you wear when you eat." Bon appetite folks.

"I often wondered why my parents called serious dating a courtship. You may not agree with my answer but I'm going to float it past you anyway." Art

RELATIONSHIP OVERHAULS

Committed couples could benefit from the mariner's annual process of assessment and renewal. If you want smooth sailing put your relationship up on blocks once a year to assess its overall condition before developing an overhaul strategy.

Observing living things spring to life after a dormant winter is one of my favorite pleasures. The Mrs. Herself and I migrate to Florida each year (cowards that we are). But like the snowbirds we've become, rush back up north to catch nature's annual coming-out party. Upon returning this year, I drove past our local yacht club. The boats were still in dry dock, looking like an unfortunate pod of beached whales rather than the picturesque fleet I knew them to be. A friend and his wife were up to their backsides in sawdust and paint chips stripping the hull of their ancient boat. The old girl they were working on (I'm referring to the boat) had been around the harbor a few times. In dry dock she looks her age but when she hits the water a radiant classic springs to life. Her owners have lovingly restored each detail. She's not as fast or as sleek as today's fiberglass models but she earns respect from passers by that is denied even the most expensive nouveau vessel.

Much can be learned about primary relationships from the process of nautical maintenance. When assessing your relationship don't forget to include less conspicuous parts that are usually below the surface. With boats and relationships there are always two factors to consider. Above the water is for comfort and show, what lies below is for safety and go.

A relationship overhaul can be enhanced by adhering to the Chinese yin/yang theory. It suggests that yin (male) force is by nature, tough and hard. It maintains life, preserves dryness, is unyielding to external force, prone to travel and obsessed with making things work. The primary focus of a yin force is procreation, productivity and fending off potential enemies. By contrast, theYang (female) force is preoccupied with preserving wellness and providing creature comforts. It strives to maintain health, create harmony, develop esthetically pleasing environments and provide life's essential (growth/creative) moisture. The mission of a yang force is to nurture.

Every human has a dominant orientation. Effective people also develop the flip side of their nature. Engaging in non traditional behaviors that break stereotype; for example; men assuming cleaning and kitchen duty or women making mechanical repairs, helps foster respect for the oft times unappreciated contribution of their partner. All aspects of humanity, be it in the kitchen or the bedroom, at work or out in the community grow and become healthier when people are willing to bend their roles.

Primary relationships are more rewarding when the full scope of each partner's potential is developed. Don't be afraid to explore your other side. Ancient Chinese wisdom dictates that yin cannot exist without yang and vice versa. Balance is the essence of becoming a whole person. They believe that centered people look above and below the waterline and are capable of building better relationships.

"Creating a positive first impression on people necessitates knowing what to say and how to present it. The challenge is monumental because everybody has a different opinion. Those who have a sixth sense about the needs of others have a distinct advantage. The rest of us could use a little help.' Art

The research of Drs. David Merrill and Roger Reid identified patterns of human behavior called Social Style. Their conclusions created a means of lowering relationship tension during interpersonal exchange. Understanding the behavioral home base of others can help you communicate more effectively.

COMMUNI-CATING WITH STYLE

Mother nature evenly distributed a variety of behavioral (methods of speech and action) characteristics across the human race. Two scales combine to identify people with differing social styles. Scale #1 (assertiveness): Draw a horizontal line. Write ask to the left of center and tell on the right. Scale # 2 (responsiveness): Draw a vertical line that evenly dissects your assertiveness scale. Write hides at the top and shows at the bottom.

Assertiveness, is determined by the degree to which a person displays asking or telling behaviors during interpersonal exchanges. Tellers are extroverts. They tend to lean forward, speak first, fast and often. Askers are introverts. They typically lean back and say more with less. Don't make the mistake of assuming that tellers are more powerful. My wife can makes a point with a simple asking phrases such as, "do you enjoy living here?" Position a significant other on the assertiveness scale, based on the behaviors they display most of the time.

Responsiveness, is determined by the degree to which a person appears reserved or openly demonstrative about how they feel. People erroneously conclude that volatility display means the sender has stronger feelings than a person who hides his or her emotion. Display is not an accurate measure of feeling intensity. Those who openly display emotions are usually more animated. They wear their heart on a sleeve and touch others with greater frequency. Now position your significant other on the responsiveness scale.

Next, name the four quadrants you just created. Upper left the deep thinker, upper right the director, lower left the relationship specialist, lower right the social coordinator. Congratulations, you have identified the behavioral home base of your significant other.

Prior to social interaction take the time to position the other person's assertiveness and responsiveness pattern. Once a home base has been determined, you can lower relationship tension for the other person by modifying the way you communicate to fit his or her way of doing things. This gesture will raise your own tension level but the odds of connecting and making a positive impact will be improved. Each behavioral home base, shares a characteristic with two other groups. Kitty corner quadrants have nothing in common with each other. These relationships are rich in diversity, supporting the adage that opposites attract. Remember that interacting with opposites will use up a great deal of energy.

Style Characteristics:

The Deep Thinker:

Preoccupied with how. Strength is organization. Afraid of making mistakes. Will avoid conflict and try to escape under pressure. Needs time to think things through. To connect with these people provide logic, accuracy, structure and security.

The Relationship specialist:

Preoccupied with why. Strength is building relationships. Concerned with offending and hurting the feelings of others. Acquiesces (goes along) under pressure. Seldom gets mad but will often get even. To connect with these people allow time for your relationship to develop before making demands.

The Director:

Preoccupied with what. Strength is getting things done. Afraid of losing control. Wants to take charge under pressure. Won't beat around the bush. Results oriented. To connect with these people use facts.

The Social Coordinator:

Preoccupied with who. Strength is entertaining. Concerned about being disliked. Will attack under pressure. Likes to be the center of attention. To connect with these people be socially active and keep the good times rolling.

Conclusion:

No quadrant is more effective than any of the others. We all know how to get things done using our natural style. Observing the behavior patterns of others will help you modify your half of a social interaction and make it easier for other people to hear, understand and enjoy dealing with you.

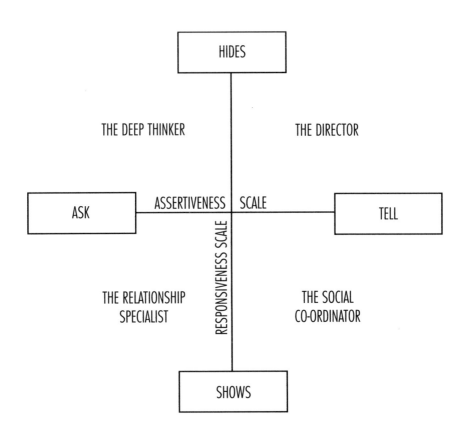

"Altruistic attitudes that provide ongoing support while demanding nothing in return from the recipient, rob people of their dignity and weakens their self-preservation instinct. Society must do more for the disadvantaged than keep them." Art

Zoos provide animal inhabitants with the necessities of life, security, food and shelter. The animal keepers are trained professionals who genuinely feel for their wards. They offer care well beyond the basics available to wild animals. Nutrition planning, medical assistance and for those who qualify as members of an endangered species, an international dating service is available.

TO KILL WITH KINDNESS

At first glance zoo residents look like they've got it made. With life's essentials assured, uncertainty eliminated and protection from predators, they have nothing to worry about. But kept animals are never happy campers. Theirs is but a demeaning facsimile of life. And it shows. Animals in captivity bear little resemblance to free ranging creatures. In the wild, life and death decisions are the norm. Animals live with the consequences of their every action. In contrast to haggard, dull eyed inmates who pace aimlessly in confined spaces, wild animals are alert and healthy. Each day they must earn the right to stay alive and even then a great deal of luck is involved. Wild animals learn from experience that there are no guarantees in nature's grand scheme.

Human institutions such as slavery, incarceration and the welfare state share a destructive common denominator that comes with dependence. Relying on someone or something other than yourself for the essentials of life is a risky business. Dependence in any form eventually makes living things lazy, unresponsive and neurotic. It is the nature of plants and animals to work at survival. Death is only one predator away. An accident or a few days without food and water means its all over. Accumulated wealth, knowledge and wisdom cannot change the mortality of living things.

The welfare state was founded on the honorable principle of helping others. But it violates a basic truth. Remove the necessity of people having to participate in their own survival and you eliminate their dignity. The wealthy may pay others to do their bidding but without having to make a personal contribution towards their own survival they become just as unhappy and unfulfilled as the unemployed. There are times when people need assistance. But the helping process should focus on stretching not shrinking recipients. A compassionate society would demand and make available the means so that citizens (within the limits of individual capacity) could participate and contribute towards their own survival. To work is not a right, it's a necessity.

"There is a healthcare battle going on. A medical monopoly is trying to exert complete authority over what I do with and choose to put into my body. And they are using my taxes to fund self serving research." Art

The history of healthcare is rife with assumed facts that crashed under closer scrutiny. For example in 1978, my doctor advised that chiropractic treatment was without merit and dangerous. Research has since vindicated spinal adjustment as the most effective means of getting people with back pain, back to work.

ALTERNATE OR COMPLE- MENTARY MEDICINE

Medical practitioners are trained and governed by institutions that are overly committed to a mechanistic perspective. They operate from an assumption that the universe is no greater than the sum of its parts and that all of life's mysteries will one day be rationalized by scientific theory. The medical establishment is a multi billion dollar industry that is assuming too much control over my life. Some health care sectors are almost God like in their zeal, assuming a thou shalt have no other Gods before me attitude. Prescription drug companies for example, relegate all but their own to the status of unethical charlatans. A powerful pharmaceutical cartel recently lobbied government to exert more control over the health food industry. They failed thank goodness. For centuries, herbs and minerals have been used by ordinary people to promote health. The popularity of natural remedies creates unwanted competition for a drug industry that has grown accustomed to having its own way.

Publicly subsidized healthcare research is conducted primarily by pharmaceutical and technology driven industries. Subsequently, medical scientists are mechanistically oriented in their attitude towards the treatment of specific disease. Their bias promotes and supports only practitioners who use and prescribe establishment products. By contrast, the perspective of physiotherapists, herbalists, acupuncturists and chiropractors et al, is holistic. They focus on prevention, wellness and self-help. Just as carpet layers pay little attention to chandeliers, mechanistic researchers discount natural or holistic solutions. Recent examples include promoting baby formula as superior to mother's milk, not disclosing that premature babies strapped close to mother's breast 24 hours a day are doing as well as premies treated with state of the art equipment or not acknowledging that the hormone melatonin can induce restful sleep and prevent jet lag.

Any treatment or remedy not administered by the medical establishment has been labeled alternate medicine. Alternate is an unfortunate choice of words because it implies an either/or solution. All facets of healthcare should be complementary not competing. We owe much to medical science and will continue to expect more. It has advanced human longevity and contained infectious disease. But because of an understandable bias, the industry is inadvertently throwing two important babies out with the bath water: #1 the value of people accepting responsibility for their own health by using preventative measures along with medical treatment. #2 the need to research and promote the inherent benefits of natural remedies and non-medical treatments.

"I remember Jimmy Durante making light of his trademarked snout by saying, only the nose knows. I've grown to appreciate how much my nose really does know" Art

The setting is a blissful spring afternoon. Yours truly is snoozing on a porch swing. Suddenly an unknown force transports me backwards in time to the seventh grade. Kids that haven't crossed my mind in 40 years are there. Jerry the scholar, competing for top honors with the passion of an NFL lineman. Evelyn, using her budding feminine wiles to embarrass the boys. And Moe, a much younger version of the real estate agent who sold my daughter her house-magically returned bow tie and all, to his past life as a school teacher.

A NOSE TO REMEMBER

How did I tap into such vivid memories and why would I return to a place I couldn't wait to get out of? On reflection, I discovered that my travel ticket was the aroma of lilacs in bloom. I remember beautiful purple and white blossoms growing outside of the open windows at my public school. Because spring lilacs heralded the arrival of summer vacation they became a powerful memory key. In those days, nature's annual lilac burst set my mind to more important things, such as baseball bats and a faithful four legged companion who played a great center field.

Nature bestowed a wonderful gift when she gave us the capability of reliving magnificent moments from our past. Having a process to access pleasant memories is a valuable asset. That's where you should let your nose butt into your business. I am a skeptic about the unsubstantiated claims made by aroma therapy advocates. A plethora of scented products claim to aid relaxation, cure depression, enhance libido and even help people connect with past lives. But I don't want to throw the baby out with the bath water. Science has validated smell as the most powerful human memory jogger. Aromas that appeal to me include:

- lilacs (aforementioned)
- popcorn (Saturday afternoon movies)
- turkey (family get togethers)
- the smell of new cars (a successful career)
- baby powder (tender moments with my children)
- my wife's perfume (candlelight and romance).

My favorite smells are tied to memorable moments. I can relive them again and again by accessing a related scent, closing my eyes and deep-breathing myself into a relaxed state. In this condition I am led down memory lane by the nose. Who would have guessed that my substantial proboscis could take me on a magic carpet ride to the past. But when you stop and think, the idea of "nose time-travel" makes scents.

I was never a scholar. A desire to please kept me near the top of the class until high school's homework regimen destroyed my work ethic (what little there was of it). At the time, doing things seemed more important than the priorities of academia.

FAILING SUCCESSFULLY

I lived for the moment as a teen, not in the past or for the future. Fortunately music fostered a burning desire to learn. French horn and trombones gave way to the guitar. Playing in a band provided an opportunity to learn, achieve, earn and find myself as a person. But freedom quickly lost its charm, as the longer-term career prospects for underage musicians became clear. Fortunately, exposure to strong family values kept me out of harm's way during these turbulent times. I sensed that my life lacked discipline and that to succeed, I'd need an education. I signed myself into a military academy to extend my academic standing, achieve a degree of financial independence, travel and acquire some discipline. It was a difficult road but it worked. From my first career failure (as a musician), I discovered the exhilaration of following a dream and how to learn from experience.

After an undistinguished military career I was encouraged by well-intentioned family members to become a machinist apprentice at a local manufacturing plant. It was a disaster. I had no mechanical aptitude whatsoever and to make matters worse, I was accident-prone. I left failure #2 after one year to become the world's worst telephone installer. During this debacle I remember concealing a wire by fishing through a closet. The customer complained a few days later because I had unwittingly drilled through a folded coffee table, permanently wiring it inside the closet. Other incidents included drilling up the center of a piano leg, falling into a rotted septic tank and several unscheduled drops from rooftops and telephone poles.

I had the lowest quality and productivity record in the company but at that point, divine intervention interceded. At the depth of my despair, management added a selling responsibility to the installation job. Most of the technicians hated selling but I flourished. Our team became top producers by defying union protocol. Secretly, I did all the selling while my technically gifted mates did the work. Discovering my latent capacity to sell opened a universe of opportunity. As a technician I was a square peg in a round hole. But later on, my value as a consultant (charged with advising management) was enhanced by the previous failures. I had lived the life of a front line employee and knew its trials and tribulations first hand. Failure becomes a gift when you learn from the experience.

I eventually made peace with academia by graduating with a Masters Degree in Applied Behavioral Science at the ripe old age of 45. Mechanical capacity still alludes me. The Mrs. Herself instinctively reaches for the first aid kit each time I pick up a tool.

"Happiness does not mean an absence of concern. People with no problems soon lose interest and become lethargic zombies. Turned on human beings select a manageable number of problems to work on and fully engage themselves in finding solutions." Art

EFFECTIVE PROBLEM SOLVING

An experiment conducted by behavioral scientists discovered that problem-solving procedures were inhibiting creative thought. Conventional methods of problem solving begin with a detailed assessment of the current situation and clarification of specific problems. Researchers assessed the enthusiasm and effectiveness of this method by measuring room sound in decibels and counting the number of negative/positive adjectives used during the problem solving discussion. They also rated the merit of solutions proposed by each study group. This experiment proved that if imagination is used before rational thinking begins, better decisions are made and participants are more committed to the outcome. Here's how it works.

Activity #1 Imagine success:

Before trying to solve a problem, imagine and discuss what it would be like once your problem has been resolved. Talk as though success has already happened. What is different now? How are you feeling about the accomplishment?

During the Second World War, an eminent social scientist, Kert Lewin, was asked to help the US Army overcome the reluctance of soldiers to eat powdered eggs. Lewin created a simple yet effective problem solving process called force field analysis. This useful tool identifies what is, by recording contributors (forces that are helping move towards a goal) and resistors (forces working against the goal). He determined that the status quo exists because the contributing and resisting forces are in balance. Add a contributor or remove a resistor and the current situation or status quo will change.

Activity #2 Document what is:

Record a summary of your imagined preferred future. Under your summary, draw a vertical line down the center of the page. Title this line status quo. Title the left half of the page contributors. Underline this heading with an arrow pointing towards the status quo line. Title the right half resistors and underline with an arrow pointing towards the status quo line. List forces that will help you move towards your goal in the contributors column and list what could hold you back under resistors. What emerges is a clear picture of your ideal, the current reality and what needs to be done to close the gap.

Those of us who have tried to live on a rigid diet have experienced the 'shoot yourself in the foot' syndrome. It happens because we try to control our behavior with contributors (i.e. rules, punishment and incentives). The uninhibited child that resides in all of us resents being should on and will eventually lash out. Lewin's breakthrough was discovering that people can move towards a goal without risking a subconscious backlash. The trick is to focus on removing or minimizing the impact of roadblock resistors, rather than adding contributors. When rules, rewards or punishments are overdone, people will sabotage even their most honorable intentions.

Activity #3 Eliminate the impact of resistors:

To begin moving towards your goal, rank order resistors in terms of their negative impact. Eliminate the easy ones first then develop an action plan for the rest. Get your rebellious child working for you by keeping the rules, incentives and punishments to a minimum.

Conclusion:

The next time you want to resolve a serious problem or make an important decision, fire up your imagination first. Create a vision of your preferred future. Then use the force field analysis process. You will be setting yourself up for success.

P.S. Lewin did resolve the Army's powdered egg issue. He surmised that the problem wasn't with taste or texture. The troop's resistor was just the thought of eating processed eggs. His surprisingly effective and simple solution was to throw a few egg shells into the powdered mix.

FORCE FIELD ANALYSIS

CONTRIBUTORS   RESISTORS

STATUS QUO

"You don't necessarily have to climb a wall or knock it down. You can also go around the structure or be content with your own side of the fence." Art

Residing by the water's edge keeps me alert to the uncontrollable spontaneity of life. Alive means facing the unexpected and perpetual change. The social scientist, Eric Fromm, suggested that people who can't be happy without neatness, organization, structure and stability; may be suffering from a mild form of necrophilia (abnormal attractions of an erotic nature towards the dead.) Such people are afraid of life's unpredictable spontaneity. They superimpose man made institutions in a fruitless effort to control nature.

GOING WITH THE FLOW

My time on the waterfront included disastrous attempts at harbor, dock and beachfront construction. Mother Nature eventually made her irrefutable point that trying to build a permanent structure on an evolving shoreline is pure folly. I learned that successful undertakings involve ongoing adjustments to accommodate the good, bad and the ugly that fate inevitably throws our way. Progress seldom moves in a straight line. Setbacks are inevitable and to succeed you must learn from experience.

The ancient Greeks were champions of linear thought. Their expectation was for continuous and direct movement towards a declared goal. Regression of any kind was considered a failure. Mythical Greek Gods may have been capable of perfection but humans then and now, will always fall short. Perfect minds, perfect bodies, perfect architecture, were noble aspirations but the unwillingness of the Greeks to accept imperfection fueled the demise of their once great empire. The Greeks were the first people to compartmentalize work as an activity removed from other parts of normal living. Prior to their contribution people just woke up and stayed busy throughout the day without worrying about labels or classification. Hebrew philosophy provides a more realistic perspective. It dictates that life has a natural ebb and flow. The challenge facing all humans is to go with the flow without losing heart or at the other extreme becoming overly optimistic. One should expect light at the end of each tunnel and reversals to both good and bad fortunes.

Failure is a precursor to success. I had the good fortune of writing a book that became a best seller. Seven publishers rejected the concept before it was finally printed. Laminated skis were discovered on the 48th try. That project translates into a failure to success ratio of 47:1. 3M's most profitable product Post it notes, came into being because an alert employee found a practical use for a new adhesive that had failed its prescribed test (it wouldn't stick permanently).

Living successfully requires going with the flow. Reject your obsession with perfection, accept what is and expect both good and bad situations to change. But most importantly, take the time to learn from experience.

"One of life's most important lessons is knowing when to hang on and when to let go." Art

> In the olden days people could afford to be callused about change because. there was fat in the system. I remember the boss coming back from a planning session all worked up about a grand solution they had worked out. We knew how to stay out of harms way and would dive under a table for two or three weeks until things got back to normal.

YOU WON'T GROW UNTIL YOU THROW SO LET GO

Every couple of hundred years or so, a human condition altering event would occur. For example, man's harnessing of fire, the wheel, telescopes and the compass (explorers couldn't have left home without that one).

Today we are confronting unprecedented change. Our challenge is a stereo mega trend. On the first track is the mind boggling advance of computing and communication speed. A prime example of the digital revolution is the internet. It's like the Klondike gold rush, wild and wooly with no rules.

On the other stereo track, Marshal McLuhen's global village is upon us. Business people, economists and politicians are trying to figure out what the old song, "he's got the whole world in his hands," really means. What we do know is that nation states no longer control or excerpt much influence over their own employ-ment climate, currency rates, stock market or trading patterns.

The following metaphore explains the impact of a stereo mega change. Accomplished sailors can handle a severe pitch (for most of us that means front to back). Nor do they have any trouble mas-tering a roll (side to side). But when the sea chops up with both pitch and roll, its called a yaw, the consequence of which is often, "over the side and every man for himself." This double-whammy causes most storm centered marine tragedies.

A new reality is that it really doesn't matter what or how much you know anymore because much of what is in your head will be out-dated before you have a chance to use it anyway. Yesterday there was an assumption that people in the know were more valuable than the rest of us. We got hired or promoted because of what we knew from experience or from our education. But today, knowl-edge can be a liability. Anybody who thinks or acts as though they know what's going on, is insane. Nobody can possibly know what a competitor on the other side of the globe did yesterday, what con-sumers are thinking about today or what they will be willing to pay tomorrow. Information is flowing so quickly, no single human being can possibly keep up. The problem with knowing is that it makes learning unnecessary. People resist change because learning screws up their assumed power base of knowing.

The impact of this stereo mega trend can't be avoided but we can do the boy scout thing and "Be Prepared". Effective preparation means shifting your paradigm (way of looking at the world). Paradigms are about pattern recognition. Unless you can see emerging patterns the whole world will appear mad. But once you get the picture, what were previously confused random events will suddenly make sense and new options will materialize.

To succeed we must make a 180 degree shift from the mindset of knowing to an attitude of not knowing. Remember-you read it here first. Those of us that don't know may actually be winning. Don't run to the bank or your boss demanding more money. Declaring, "I haven't got a clue" will not bring on a hallaluya chorus. All you really need to know about change is that, "your knowing mindset must be replaced with a not knowing attitude plus a process for finding out and taking action faster than the competition.

The individual is an irrelevant unit of society. Things start happening only when one makes a connection with other people, places or things. What exists inside a single head or heart is just a figment of imagination until it gets expressed and noticed by others. The relationship others have with you develops exclusively from the signals you send.

SIGNAL SENDING

Attila the Hun, (and perhaps his mother) felt that he was generally misunderstood and deep down, really quite a nice guy. The oft-used phrase, "You just have to get to know him," didn't apply in Attila's case because nobody got to live that long.

If your beliefs and feelings are not translated into signals that others can decipher, nothing of significance will happen. Signal sending is critical to parents because children haven't fully developed their verbal capacity. They pay more attention to what moms and dads do than what is said. I would rather see a sermon than hear one any day. In my world, action speaks louder than words.

Values and vision (what you believe in and where you want to go) may be clear in your mind, but if they aren't expressed by observable actions, you will never attract supporters. A pitiful sight is watching people trying lead when they have no ability to attract followers.

I was facilitating a values clarification workshop with executives responsible for Canada's air traffic control system, when two senior officers had a priorities squabble. Life and death issues were involved. One executive was responsible for technology and the other managed the human resource. They had tried to negotiate but couldn't come up with a mutually satisfactory resolution. The pair asked their leader to arbitrate. Rather than make a decision he asked, "what are our core values?" The technical leader retorted that he didn't have time to play around. "We need a decision and we need one quick," was their bottom line. But the leader dug in his heels. "If you really believe in the core values we just clarified, they'll serve as a third person in the room and help the two of you find a solution that fits." He held their toes to the fire until they came up with an acceptable resolution.

The senior manager could have gone on talking about the importance of values as a decision making tool. Instead, he used a serious incident as a catalyst for on-the-job learning. A powerful signal sent at a critical time, drove the message home. Both directors learned from the experience and shared the benefits of the process with the troops. The leader's stock went up because he signaled an unconditional commitment to the organization's core values.

In Spokane Washington, I had the good fortune of being introduced to a consulting group called The center for Work and the Human Spirit. They provided me with the following productive insight.

FEELING FROM ANOTHER WORLD

No matter what the situation or event, two distinct happenings occur in unison. The first affects your position or role as a customer, parent, student, manager, friend or spouse. The second impacts you as the person behind your position or role.

Imagine yourself standing waist deep in water. As you do a 360 degree turn, you notice boats, swimmers, water fowl and waves. Next, imagine yourself donning a face mask and snorkel. Once your mask is lowered beneath the surface, a new reality suddenly appears. Prior to putting your mask in the water, you were not consciously aware of the world existing below the waterline.

Above the waterline represents tangible things, places and materials. This world is associated with WHAT happens. Below the waterline deals with HOW things are handled. It is a less visible world concerned with feelings, attitudes and beliefs.

Many people charge through life producing, creating and measuring success exclusively to above the waterline standards. Others are overly sensitive to events happening on the surface and become overwhelmed.

At the heart of every organization and family is a complex network of interpersonal relationships. The difference between an excellent and non-contributing relationship, at home, at work or out in the community; is the willingness and ability of people to attend to both above and below the waterline issues. When one perspective is dominant people are less effective. For example, dysfunction occurs when people:

1. Become overly preoccupied with the feelings of self or others, at the expense of getting things done.
2. Get things done at the expense of someone else, with little regard for their feelings.

"I often reflect on why I got together with my wife and how we have managed to stay together this long. There were early warnings that ours would be an eventful marriage." Art

MARITAL OMENS

I attended a military academy on the west coast. After six months of training, the brass finally granted a day pass with a restriction to remain within 10 miles of the base. I paid no attention to the order and hitchhiked with a fellow cadet to his home, well over 100 miles away. During those few hours of freedom, I met my future wife. [Omen #1 Our relationship began during a violation of military law]

We dated for five years before getting married. The wedding was to be held in my wife's church but in my home town. The priest and I had met previously during a mandatory check of my readiness (and worthiness) to marry a member of his flock. I recall our wedding rehearsal as intimidating. My wife remembers it as embarrassing. I tried to lighten up our somewhat reserved priest by asking, "We've already gone through the ceremony, what would it cost to have you sign the papers and call this marriage a done deal?" To make matters worse, I quipped, "I'd sleep better tonight if you did." Omen #2...[My sense of humor was not shared by everybody-the Mrs. included]

A newly appointed Mrs. Herself and I worried about being the brunt of pranks from my raucous buddies. After the wedding we changed our plans and drove to the privacy of a remote country inn. It was noon before we remembered the necessity of food. Still aglow, we sheepishly herded our rumpled selves to the dining room. When our eyes finally left each other my wife and I discovered in horror; my mother, father, mother in law, sisters and an assortment of aunts and uncles, sitting in the next booth. They smiled and nodded knowingly. The newlyweds responded with a crimson blush.

Omen #3 [We knew our family would be extended by marriage, we just didn't expect them to show up the very next day.}

Our first vacation as a married couple was to the home of my mother-in-law. She went out of her way to make us feel comfortable. We tried to resist using the master bedroom but mother would have no part of her eldest daughter sleeping in a guest room. Exhausted from travelling all day, we asked to be excused early in the evening. My wife's family smiled and nodded knowingly a second time. Their antics no longer bothered us because we had a few months of married life under our belts. My wife was already asleep when I finally collapsed into the bed. Having no previous experience at accommodating 200 pound males, the bed collapsed under the sudden strain. We found ourselves lying on the floor in a tangled mess of bedposts, sheets and frilly pink pillows. A moment of deathly silence concluded when downstairs a chorus of cheers emanated from our family's overactive imagination.

Omen #4 [Sometimes the innocent appear guilty. Unfortunately I've never mastered the reverse]

As the initial omens predicted, ours has been an eventful marriage. It has thrived primarily because my mate has a forgiving nature and a wonderful sense of humor.

"We deny ourselves one of life's most pleasurable experiences when we fail to laugh heartily. I've noticed myself responding with polite chuckles or a silent grin to situations that would have doubled me over in the old days." Art

LAUGH STYLES

A "life is not something to laugh at" message has somehow permeated our collective psyche. We have become a nation that would rather spectate than participate. People aren't laughing as much because they are satisfied with listening to people on TV laugh for them (usually a canned laugh track). Couch potato viewing makes Jack a dull boy and the Jerry Springer show does little to lighten up Jill's demeanor.

As herding creatures, human beings are genetically conditioned to pick up on what's happening around them. Being around people who laugh heartily and often is essential to good health and emotional wellness. Gaiety is more contagious than stoic behavior so it makes sense to seek out those already infected with the laughter bug. Or better yet, become a carrier yourself and spread the laughter virus around. Children (and uptight adults) need to see more grown-ups sharing the gift of contagious merriment. Do yourself and others a great favor. Laugh out loud when you are in a crowd. Can you find your uninhibited, fun-loving self in one of the following laugh styles?

The belly laugh:

This often silent but never discreet favorite is the most energetic of all laugh styles. It usually ends with the practitioner grabbing their midsection and doubling over in the proverbial, "I'm going to be sick," posture. During extended spasms, belly laughers have a propensity to piddle. This is particularly true of vintage practitioners.

The wheezer laugh:

It is difficult to resist the urge to perform a Heimlich first aid maneuver during this most peculiar laugh style. Wheezers get red-faced and often appear incapable of drawing another breath. But eventually a giant sucking sound signals they have survived yet another convulsion. This laugh sometimes ends in a spasmodic coughing bout.

The nostril laugh:

The aristocracy invented the lost etiquette of snuff sneezing. They probably originated this oft-times messy laugh style. The process begins with a rigorous clenching of the jaw. Next, all body orifices (except for the nose) slam shut. Violent air bursts erupt in rapid succession through a pulsating proboscis. Muffled sounds resembling chairs being dragged across a hardwood floor resonate deep within the laugher's sinus cavities. It is wise to stand well back of nostril laughers during the cold and allergy season.

"Being anointed with the title 'mover and shaker' is not always a term of endearment." Art

Some people are born with nomadic tendencies while others stick close to their roots. When people like me attend a local ballgame, they don't know if they should be watching home or visitors on the scoreboard. I am a genetic hybrid who displays equal homer and wandering characteristics. In other words I want to have my cake and eat it too.

THE MOVING EXPERIENCE

Mixed homer/nomadic genes produce complications for their owner. When I travel it takes a great deal of time at the destination before I can relax. A colleague told me to walk around the block before retiring in a strange hotel. My dog makes similar rounds when she arrives anywhere. The personal touch using nature's magic marker establishes her boundaries. Once the piddling is complete my dog curls up contentedly like she never left home. In spite of the K9 success formula, modesty, hygiene and bladder size preclude my participating in full-monty walk-arounds.

The necessity to sell and buy real estate each time we moved has been a challenge for my family. I was told by an accomplished agent to heat a small amount of vanilla extract on an open burner before potential buyers toured a house. This tactic produces an aroma of fresh baking that can make a New York apartment smell like Grandma Walton's kitchen. But there can be serious side effects. I gained 40 pounds when a property didn't sell for six months. My eating was influenced more than the prospect's urge to buy.

During a cross-country move we stopped for the night in Minnesota. My oldest daughter was jubilant. She had just lost a tooth and was fanaticizing falling into big bucks. She was worried that the tooth fairy would not make it past hotel security. We finally convinced her that desk clerks were no match for a committed fairy. Our curious three year old, wanting to get in on the payoff, couldn't understand why her teeth could not be extracted on demand, "Nanny takes hers out every night," she lamented. Daughter #1 eventually curled up with a spent molar under her pillow.

The Mrs. Herself and I were rudely awakened the next morning by a mournful ululate, "my tooth's gone and the fairy didn't leave any money." Being on intimate terms with the tooth fairy I knew something was awry. Circumstantial evidence and a guilty face identified our three-year-old as the culprit. During the night she had discovered loose change under her sister's pillow. She stood on a chair to unlock a security chain, opened a dead-bolted door and walked down the hall past twenty five rooms to a soft drink dispenser. Our 30 inch child then managed to deposit several coins and buy a soda. She returned to the scene of the crime without waking anybody, re locked the door (including the security chain), finished her drink and went back to sleep. Her only mistake was failing to retrieve change from the machine. This stranger than fiction fairy tale remains a favorite moving story in the McNeil family.

P.S.

Daughter # 1 the gal who worried about her money now works for a bank. Daughter #2 who almost pulled off a perfect crime at age of 3 works in the security department of a transportation company. Who says destiny doesn't reside in the genes?

" I love the game and I enjoy the players but hate my inability to master its many complexities." Art

Tennis whites, leisurely games played in a posh club where spectators sip cool drinks and everybody looks like a movie star. Hello! That's not the tennis environment I play in. My gang bears no resemblance to the above-mentioned daydream (where nobody ever sweats and everybody has a perfect backhand). But this great game can handle reality so dear reader, I'm going to expose you to the cold hard facts as I know them.

TENNIS ANYONE

Tennis aficionados are a tad peculiar. Initially I was confused by the game's scoring system. After my first court experience I blurted out, "Honey, I finally get it-love means nothing." The Mrs. Herself wouldn't speak to me for a week. Another strange feature in tennis scoring is that rather than count 1,2,3 like a normal game, the progression goes 15, 30, 45, deuce and advantage. Since nobody seems to know why, I developed a theory. The people who authored the game rules eventually grew too old to play a full match and eliminated 42 of the middle points.

As a snowbird, one of life's little pleasures is the opportunity to play tennis year-round. But Florida tennis is not a pretty sight. The million-dollar man would not stand-out if he visited my club because our players are adorned with high-tech devices on their knees, ankles, wrists, elbows and backs. Before each game everything that moves is covered with support bandages. Some look like Egyptian mummies. I've only witnessed one senior who played exposed (in Florida a senior is anybody over the age of 85-unless there's a meal or admission discount). This elderly man hits the court every day without a single wrap. It isn't that he is in particularly good shape it's because his joints won't move at all. He stands anchored in the classic ready position for the entire game while his partner plays around him. He gets his exercise changing ends. I've never seen him run or bend over. He's deadly however, if you hit a ball directly at him. This man talks about his stroke (nothing to do with tennis) and can serve without looking up at the ball. But he loves the game, is a good sport and can give as good as he gets.

Most Florida tennis clubs are matriarchal societies. Females typically outnumber the males, are in better shape and usually run the place. Women command the best court times and decide who will play with who in mixed doubles. Enthusiastic ladies actually carry their balls (tennis) under a tennis skirt. A noticeable gender difference is that when women play tennis, they laugh more than men. The frivolity often causes rookie males to assume that the ladies are not taking the game seriously. During a low-key sociable mixer, I was taken aside by my partner (a pleasant looking lady who bore a striking resemblance to Aunt Bea from the Andy Griffith show). With a beautiful smile she whispered, "don't let Lucy's limp influence your serve, aim a few hard ones to her left side-she's got a bad hip."

"It's a great feeling to find yourself playing over your head. Unfortunately for those (of us) who don't practice, it happens seldom or not at all." Art

Believers call it 'grace', physiologists call it 'being centered' and athletes refer to it as the 'zone'. There are many names for this special state when for brief interludes, people are capable of performing beyond their natural capability.

GETTING THE ZONE MESSAGE

I first experienced the zone as a fastball pitcher. On rare occasions for some unknown reason, I would shake off my catcher's signals and demand a different selection. The process was almost (but not quite) subconscious. Everything appeared to slow down. I was acutely aware of miniscule deficiencies in the batter's stance. My mind would race ahead and with breath taking clarity, envision the execution of a perfect pitch. My body would access a hidden reserve of talent and power and a pitch would unfurl exactly as I had imagined it. As if looking at slow motion through a telephoto lens, I remember seeing the seams of a fast moving baseball float past the futile swings of batters. My zone experiences produced a couple of no-hitters but for the rest of my career, more often than not, I got knocked out of the park.

I've had a few 'zone' experiences during my speaking engagements. When it happens, I feel outside of myself, listening along with the audience to an articulate flow of information that I've never heard before. Breakthrough moments are completely out of my control. They typically herald the creation of an insight that transforms my work and moves me into a different space. Perhaps this is what the clergy refer to as a state of 'grace'.

Such happenings are infrequent but life-altering when they do occur. Being prepared, informed and open to new possibilities appears to be an essential condition before a 'zone' experience will happen. Following an experience of 'grace' in 1987, I wrote my first book. To my surprise it became an international best seller. The "I" of the Hurricane was an expression of my inhibited spirituality. I have written several books since then, none of which tapped an external source for inspiration. They were works of the head, not the heart. Hopefully, one day I will be blessed again.

"The hurryider I go the behinder I get." Art

Have you noticed that time passes at an ever-increasing speed as we age? I remember leaving school for summer break. Those 2 blissful months seemed to roll on forever. Summer was such an extended interval that I worried about not remembering what I'd learned the previous year.

TIME FLIES

Another example happened during family auto trips. A familiar refrain coming from the back seat every five minutes (are we there yet?), drove me around the bend.

There's a reason for the illusion of time accelerating with age. A 5 year-old remembers against a memory bank that totals 1825 days. At 50 years of age, a personal data bank registers 18,250 days. In this example, the child experiences 24 hours as being 10 times longer than the adult. Now you know why kids get antsy when grown-ups make them wait.

Not only does time appear to accelerate with age, it veritably flies when you are having fun or completely engrossed in a pleasurable activity. When an activity captures a person's undivided attention, time-consciousness is lost. A cherished hobby, an interesting discussion between friends, a good book or challenging work project, often leaves us wondering, "where did the day go?" This phenomenon occurs because the mind is preoccupied and not reflecting against stored history. Humans create in the 'here and now' where time is less relevant. Engaging children in creative activity is a great antidote for impatience. Perhaps a subconscious desire to slow things down influences adults to engage in less interesting pastimes.

Time drags for me when the Mrs. Herself drags out her 'honey do' list. Household chores cause me to revert to a childlike state (procrastination). I was amazed to learn that a broken cupboard door had been on her top-ten list for two years. She wasn't amused when I suggested the unattended task had been assigned to me a couple of weeks ago.

Language also reminds us that time marches on. In my day most expressions were animal based. Strong as a horse, dumb as an ox, stubborn as a mule, smart as a fox, eyes like an eagle, drinks like a fish to name a few. Today's sayings are high tech. For example, turned on, turned off, wired, spaced out or going ballistic.

Where will tomorrow's language take us and, "are we there yet?"

THE RESPITE

My buddies and I meet a couple of times a week for lunch or a coffee. They are busy local business owner/managers and periodically getting away from the public is a welcomed stress reducer. My problem is just the opposite. Sitting in front of a computer all day (particularly when my writing is not going well) feels like being in a sensory depravation chamber. During bouts of writer's block, I've gone so far as to leave messages on my answering machine to hear a human voice. When I start saying thank you to a computer for reminding me that, "your Email files are using excess space," I know it's time for a break.

We alternated between several eating establishments until we met a lady affectionately referred to as Maw. This mother of a local restaurateur loved her job. She had the rare knack of knowing how to serve humanity as well as food, was a notorious prankster and a proverbial fountain of good will. On one occasion the boys were ribbing her about a burned out light above our corner table. She resolved the problem by delivering (with great ceremony), a cupcake with one flaming birthday candle and, to the delight of other patrons, a boisterous retort, "this will do until you guys find something else to complain about." Maw could take as good as she gave and was not above rapping violators of political correctness across the back of the head, even when an off colored story made her laugh. Another endearing quality was a penchant for laughing uncontrollably at her own jokes.

One day we arrived at the restaurant expecting the usual serving of fun and frivolity to find everybody in an uncharacteristicly somber mood. Our benefactor had been in a car accident and was fighting for her life in a critical care ward. Her daughter gave us the devastating prognosis, "they say that even if Maw lives she'll never walk again and only God knows if there is permanent brain damage." The boys and I were stunned. We sent flowers and consoled the distraught family as best we could. After the initial shock wore off we felt a huge vacuum in our stress breaks and regressed to the old pattern of rotating lunch venues. But it didn't help, something was still missing. This special lady had been providing the secret herbs and spices that made our time together special. Without her, restaurants replenished our bodies but did nothing for our souls. A few months later (after an unending stream of surgeries) the news about Maw's condition was gloomy. I traveled south on my annual snowbird migration and lost touch.

I returned home in the spring and took a nostalgic stroll up mainstreet to Maw's restaurant. It was a sad experience because I didn't recognize any of the servers. They were professional and courteous but the place didn't feel the same. I quietly adjusted my expectations, sipped a coffee and buried myself in a newspaper. Suddenly a booming voice reverberated off the walls, "where have you been?" I turned to see a familiar smiling face. It was Maw, hobbling towards me without the aid of a cane, wearing a leg cast that weighed at least as much as her. The lady's energy was infectious. " I can't wait to get back to work, I'm tired of people telling me what I'm capable of and I need a good joke, heard anything lately?" The old magic returned and I left the restaurant renewed in mind, body and spirit.

"Touchy feely activity bothered me until I discovered that people who resist are the ones who need a hug the most." Art

Outside of my immediate family, yours truly seldom initiates hugs. I fail to act on the impulse to express affection because at times the feeling isn't recognized until an opportunity has passed me by.

MY HUGGING HANDICAP

I'm not proud of this inhibition because I enjoy receiving hugs and understand their value to emotional health. When offered the gift of a heartfelt hug I experience a feeling of wellbeing. But it wasn't always that way. At one time I'd tense up during arrival and departure rituals, particularly during echo exchanges (an abbreviated rerun of the entire visit as the guests are leaving.) In a crowded vestibule one hugger can infect a whole gaggle of people. To the inhibited, huggers look like sharks on a feeding frenzy. After 3 or 4 seconds of embracing, I remember feeling like a trapped mouse in a room full of cats. A mysterious back-patting reflex would take over, making it look like I was trying to relieve the hugger of trapped gas. I developed a safe distance 'bend forward from the waist' handshake to defend myself against huggers. It took 4 decades for me to grow out of my inhibition. The female side of my family were (and still are) gifted huggers but my male role models were reserved when it came to emotional display.

At 45 years of age I did mid career graduate studies in the applied behavioral sciences. The campus was an uninhibited hugging community because everybody was a psychology student. The more you resisted these emerging practitioners, the more they sought you out. Eventually I learned to receive hugs with enthusiasm. I must have failed "initiating 101' however because to this day, I find myself repressing the desire to offer a hug. I often reflect on exchanges with my daughters and realize too late that I could have, should have and really wanted to hug them. A sad reality is that once you are type cast as a reluctant hugger, people keep their distance out of respect. The good news is that hugs are like boomerangs (start throwing them around and they come back in droves).

People crave contact with other living things because we are herding creatures at heart. Without touch, humans suffer the many ills of "dis-ease." Children in understaffed Romanian orphanages for example, failed to develop physically, mentally or emotionally because they did not experience sufficient human contact. Adults need human affection as well. Society has programmed us to unconditionally hug children and animals but many people cringe at the thought of hugging adults other than their partners. Seniors, as they lose close friends and family are deprived of affection they have grown accustomed to. Depriving aging adults of human contact is cruel and disrespectful.

There are hugging hypocrites out there who offer the illusion of affection. They dispense cheek pecks that climax in mid air, giving the appearance that they fear catching a disease. Another variety of emotional hypocrite is the "I have a willing mind but want no part of your body," 'A' frame hugger. These people limit contact to above the shoulder. I'd rather experience a sincere handshake than these sterile hugging facsimiles. I recognize my hugging handicap and am working hard to overcome it. Self-disclosure makes it open season for me, both as a hugger and as a hugee.

Be prepared if I meet you on the street.

Consider the following guidelines: survival = 3 hugs per day, growth = 6 hugs per day, wellness = 9 hugs per day. And remember the adage, "it is better to give than to receive."

"On the road again was a popular song but living on the road was not a pleasant experience. I survived by mastering the survival skills of a road warrior." Art

At one time my work involved extensive travel. I honed the travel process to a science, learning how to manipulate ticket agents, rack up frequent flyer points and gain access to VIP lounges. But most importantly, I learned how to survive an emergency.

CONFESSIONS OF A ROAD WARRIOR

I developed an instinct about when and where to line up during flight cancellations, learned how to pick hotels and sniff out a good place to eat. In short, I mastered the knack of commanding and receiving service excellence. My sob stories have brought tears to the eyes of hard-hearted ticket agents around the world.

But unfortunately my system breaks down when I travel with family. As a tourist, I am consistently outperformed by novices like the Mrs. Herself. Business class acumen and road warrior survival tactics, spell the kiss of death when they are used in the real world. My wife succeeds by following instructions to the letter. She has a lower service expectation, forgets about time and adopts a "when in Rome, do as the Romans do" attitude. At first glance, compliance is the key to successful tourist travel. But sometimes business travel experience can be an asset.

During a memorable family trip, a severe winter storm fowled our plane change in Atlanta. I was worried about my daughter who was 7 months pregnant at the time. Thousands of travelers were lined up trying to reschedule their cancelled flights. The airport was a zoo. There were no hotels rooms available, the restaurants and washrooms were full and disgruntled passengers were getting nasty. The thought of my daughter having to over-night in one of those uncomfortable airport chairs with a curved bottom (designed to eject people should they fall asleep) was unacceptable so I jumped the ticket counter queue. A phalanx of angry travelers objected profusely and summarily dismissed me to the back of the line. My family accepted this fate and began looking for vacant floor space to set up camp for the evening.

As a seasoned road warrior I was not about to go down without a fight. I picked the most matronly looking ticket agent, took my daughter in tow and elbowed our way up the line, pointing to daughter's delicate condition and shouting, " we have an emergency in the making here." A number of supportive strangers (probably empathetic fathers and grandfathers) began operating like a police escort, clearing the way and silencing the dissidents. My tactic worked and we were rescheduled on the next available flight. My wife and daughter although appreciative of the outcome were not enamoured with my aggressiveness. They wouldn't walk with me until we left the airport. My son-in-law appreciated the initiative and treated me like a folk hero for the rest of the trip.

"It's nice to know there are choices when it comes time to cleaning up your act."
Art

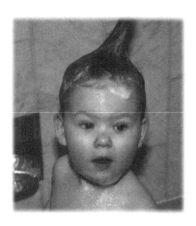

TO BATHE
OR SHOWER

After serious consideration I have concluded there is no best way to clean the human body. Determining the superiority of a bath over a shower is complex because people often try to satisfy more than ablution requirements. A host of factors can shape one's preference. The following are secondary considerations that can influence one's selection.

When looking for privacy, relaxation, staying warm, easing aches & pains or play, a bath wins hands down:

One of life's little pleasures is closing the door on a demanding world and submerging tired old bones in hot water. English bath-tubs are best because they hold the heat and are designed to accommodate long intervals of full body lounging. Room temperature is chilly in the UK, so covering yourself with hot water makes sense. Rather than heat houses to North American standards, the clever British provide electric towel warmers. Along with their deep, lengthy tubs, I considered the British towel heater a world-class innovation (until I bent over trying to dry myself in a tiny English loo and burned my backside).

North American tubs have little in common with the shape or needs of the human body. They are too short, too wide (designers must be taking body size projections from the fast food industry) and too shallow (the overflow drain takes over before half my body is immersed). Books have become my preferred tub accessory, replacing rubber ducks except for stressful occasions when I use my grandchildren's tub toys as therapy tools.

To accommodate secondary considerations such as singing, cleaning up and speed, the shower is a stand alone winner:
Singing from a sitting position in a bathtub is ineffective because one's air disbursement is unmanageable. (I am not referring to conventional problems with bath bubbles). Proper breathing is enhanced in the upright position. The echo chamber quality of a shower stall adds power to the untrained voice.

From the perspective of good housekeeping, showers eliminate those embarrassing bathtub rings and make it almost impossible for the authority figure in your life to prove that you are not cleaning up after yourself.

For intimacy & grooming needs, the bath and shower are tied neck and neck:
Ecologists (or was it the hippies?) coined a phrase, "shower with a friend and save the planet." Communal showers may save the planet but together-tubbing has saved many a marriage. In the early years, I enjoyed the taking of a luxurious tub with my wife. Advancing age made the process of getting it all together in a tub increasingly difficult. At my age it is almost impossible to unhook from spousal tub entanglements. In the beginning the Mrs. Herself and I enjoyed the contorted body contact of a shared bath. Now the experience leaves us feeling crowded, inefficient and unsafe. I favor the more tranquil act of sudsing and massaging my partner in the shower. It is less painful, ends quickly and body parts don't shrivel like they do from a prolonged tub exposure.

"Sometimes even the best laid plans go wrong." Art

While watching a program about the destruction of rain forests I had a flashback to the day Mikey and I felled a tree at our family cottage.

TIMBER TROUBLES

It began with my teenage daughters complaining bitterly about a monster tree that was blocking their access to the sun's tanning rays. Not being a sun worshipper myself, a shady cottage deck was an asset, not a liability. When confronted with repeated requests to remove the tree, I assumed what Mohamed Ali called a "rope-a-dope" strategy. I did nothing and hummed a lot. This effective technique exudes compassion and shows interest but is void of commitment. It worked definitely but not indefinitely. Unfortunately, the old tree started to show signs of aging. The transition had not registered with me because I've conditioned myself to ignore the indicators of aging, (like the arthritis that causes my pinky finger to point sideways when I tilt a teacup.)

The girls renewed their efforts and petitioned mother to have old faithful removed for safety reasons. "That tree could fall on us this very weekend," they wailed in unison. I knew it was serious because my daughters could never agreed on anything. I retired to the comfort of my shady deck, trusting the tirade would blow over long before my favorite tree. Smelling that first blood had been drawn with the safety angle, the girls intensified their assault. Finally I conceded and agreed that the tree should come down. I did not however, specify a start date.

My parents, sister and brother in law were visiting a few weeks later. The girls, sensing that an audience might translate into opportunity, played a full court press. They suggested that Mikey help me fell the tree. Not having been married long enough to recognize that a procrastination tactic was in effect, my brother in law broke ranks and agreed to participate. My last line of defense crumbled when a chain saw was deposited unceremoniously into my lap.

Because the tree was in close proximity to the cottage, I had to ensure that it would fall out of harms way. Mikey explained that direction could be controlled by cutting a 'V' on one side of the trunk and sawing from the other side. I wasn't completely convinced, so for insurance I tied a rope around the treetop. I had to connect a second length because the initial piece wasn't long enough. I went on to saw a perfect 'V', recruited the whole family to pull on the rope and began executing the final cut. Seconds before the saw broke through, the rope let go (I never earned a scout knot badge) piling my disgruntled family in a multi-generational heap. The tree snapped back like a sling-shot, crashed into the cottage, wiping out the chimney and a sizable portion of the roof. I spent the next week removing the downed tree and repairing the cottage. The girls (without a thank you) oiled up and for the next ten years, took control of what became a sun deck. I added air conditioning and spent more time indoors. My grown up daughters are now complaining about their kids having to play under UV rays on our sunlit deck. Fathers may know best, but they seldom win.

A TV action series from the 70's had its leader repeat a weekly throw-away line. "Don't you just love it when a plan comes together," was used during chaotic action scenes when Mr. T and his pals were frantically innovating to meet unforeseen circumstances.

I LOVE IT WHEN A PLAN COMES TOGETHER

There is a fundamental truth behind the premise that was presented by this TV show. Skill, trust in one's teammates, following a disciplined process and lots of practice makes it possible, not only for The A Team but for any committed group to successfully execute challenging missions; even when the unexpected happens and people have to ad lib.

I recently witnessed a plan coming together. After 4 months of arduous practice, a community production company that I had joined, staged a musical review. This was my first theatrical involvement. I am an experienced public speaker but as a singer and dancer I was uncertain, unskilled and uncoordinated.

During my audition the selection team saw enough to suspect there might be a pony under what was a raw pile of performance chaos. The troop's patience and support, plus director Ron and producer Margie's effective blend of challenge and nurture (kind of a tough cop-soft cop routine), transformed me from feeling like a horse's rear to believing in ponies.

In the beginning only the producer and director could visualize the end result the troop was working towards. I was overwhelmed as the group struggled with dance routines, complex rhythms and the close harmonies of the big band era. Veterans had to shore up anxious rookies like myself. They encouraged us to stop worrying and focus on doing the best we could; one small step at a time. My first thought after experiencing the dress rehearsal was, "I just love it when a plan comes together".

I learned the following from this wonderful experience:

- Contributing time and talents to a non-profit project, (proceeds from the show went to Save the children) can enrich the soul, strengthen a community and add a sense of wellbeing.
- Many adults subconsciously mask their fear of failure by not attempting anything new. Stretching the envelope will resurrect a "can do" attitude and help old dogs learn new tricks.
- When you think big and have the patience to step small, good things will happen.
- Stage magic was the sweet icing but the cake's recipe consisted of vision, leadership, trust, support, talent and lots of hard work.

"Many adults quit trying new things because they are afraid of making a fool of themselves. The best antidote for this stifling mindset is learning to laugh at yourself," Art

TO SPECTATE OR PARTICIPATE

The Great Lakes provide a beautiful backdrop for many fond memories during my childhood. My young adult years however, were spent on the bald headed prairies. Early exposure left me with a great affection for water but nothing in the way of mariner skill. The largest vessel I ever captained was a two person canoe. Even then, I had trouble controlling a mutinous first mate. (The Mrs. Herself has since retitled herself only mate.)

Within months of returning to my Great Lakes roots, I acquired a motor cruiser and began the arduous task of learning to master North America's tricky inland sea. I relied heavily on friends, most of whom were accomplished sailors. After two brief lessons, my buddies hung the nickname "Captain Crunch" on me. To make matters worse, they mounted a plaque to that effect in the cabin of my boat. I was accused of being so un-nautical that I believed Mobey Dick to be a venereal disease. There are sea faring genes in my makeup but making them wake up and go to work was an arduous task.

Insights gained during my induction to boat piloting:

- It is never too late to engage in a learning experience, particularly if it is associated with something you loved as a child.
- Fear of failure and its subsequent embarrassment is understandable but not lethal. Life is not a spectator sport. Woody Allen said

that success is 95 percent showing up. Inhibition is a detriment to effective living.

- During the customary awkward phase of a learning experience, remember that people will laugh with, not at you-provided you know how to laugh at yourself.

- Equipment, handbooks, specialty clothing, classroom instruction and professional coaching, mean nothing without the courage to try, fail, get up and try again... and again... and again.

- Serendipity means having an unexpected pleasant happening occur while you are in the process of doing something else. Couch potatoes have no access to serendipity because to experience it, you must be out there.

As captain of my little boat, I continue to learn from experience. To the delight of my mariner friends, I still provide more than my fair share of guffaws. An old Mennonite saying does a nice job of wrapping it up. "Life is a tough teacher because she gives a test first and the lesson later."

BOOKS AND TAPES
by Art McNeil

Leadership: The 'I' of the Hurricane (paperback or audio tape)
Contrasts management-the position with leadership-the activity.
Explains how to create will to win and the desire to belong.
A new mindset for winners (audio tape)
Shows how to replace the mindset of knowing with an attitude of
not knowing; plus a process for finding out and taking action faster
than the competition.
People and Power Shifts: beyond the trauma of restructuring
(audio tape)

Adapt	profit from Personal and Corporate change
Trust	reap unbridled power that comes with mature trust
Work	build synergy with a "street smart" partner chain
Invest	earn a fair rate of return on intellectual capital
Create	processes for finding out and taking action
Team	master the skills needed for transient teaming
Learn	benefit from the experience of yourself and others

**Life is not a Spectator Sport:How to get it on with life, rather
than just getting by** (paperback) Insight, humor and family values
designed to get you off the couch and onto the playing field of life-
building stronger relationships, a caring family, supportive communities and a successful career. (book or audio tape)

Work in progress

People and power shifts: beyond the trauma of restructuring
(paperback)

The Pinstripe Messiah (a novel)
A businessman confronts the establishment as he tries to make the
world a better place. Set around the drama of NAFTA negotiations
and the downsizing of government.

Keynote Speaking topics

Leadership the creation of will to win and desire to belong

A new mindset for winners how to Replace the mindset of knowing with an attitude of not knowing plus a process for finding out and taking action faster than the competition

People and Power Shifts beyond the trauma of restructuring

Life is not a Spectator Sport insight, humor and family values to help you get off the couch and onto the playing field of life, building successful careers, stronger relationships and supportive communities.

Art McNeil is represented by The National Speakers Bureau.
To find out more or to inquire about Art's availability as a keynote speaker for your next conference, visit The Gallery of paradigm busters at www.artmcneil.com on the internet